walking in
KINGDOM
POWER

A 60-DAY DEVOTIONAL TO
REACH YOUR DESTINY

JOE JOE DAWSON

INTRODUCTION

Destiny! The first time I heard this word something went off in my spirit and shook my soul. There's just something about this word that has always captivated me. God has created each and every person with a breathtaking destiny. This is not something you inherited from your family or can be determined by where you come from. It is something simply given to you by God. Many times in our lives, we will feel like there is something greater we are supposed to be doing with our life. This is our destiny pulling us. The happiest people are the ones who have found their God-given destiny and are living their lives to the fullest.

Many years ago, my grandmother gave me an old dictionary from the 1800s. She told me to look up some of my favorite words. Immediately I went to the word destiny, and the definition was "invincible necessity." We know there is only one thing invincible in this world and that's God. The word necessity means that it must happen. So when you look at the word destiny, it means that God has a plan for your life that absolutely must happen. God's destiny for your life is invincible. Nothing can stop it! The world will be a better place when you reach your full potential in God.

My prayer for you is that as you read this 60-day devotional you will begin to understand that God has a call upon your life that is invincible. It is mandatory. And it is very important that it comes to pass. When you know in your heart that you can do all God has called you to do, you will start to jump levels as you walk in Kingdom power. This book is meant to challenge you and equip you to keep moving forward, every day of your life, until you hit the mark that God has set before you.

Everything that has happened to you up until this point was leading you closer to the destiny that God has placed upon your life. Every day that you do not break, you are one step closer to your breakthrough. Even if things do not look bright right now, remember when you call upon the Lord He will move on your behalf. I can promise you that God is doing more for you behind the scenes than you could ever imagine. When God places destiny upon a person, it is because He needs that dream manifested on the earth. God wants you to succeed in life more than you do. You reaching your destiny and fulfilling His dream for your life was His plan from the beginning. Be encouraged, my friends! I pray that *Walking in Kingdom Power* will help launch you deeper into the things God has destined you to do.

WALKING IN KINGDOM POWER

Devotion 1

Matthew 6:6 "But you, when you pray, go into your room, and when you have shut your door, pray to your Father who is in the secret place; and your Father who sees in secret will reward you openly." (NKJV)

This is one of the most personal and intimate scriptures in all of Scripture. These red letters flowing with love clearly state eight times that Jesus is calling you to a closer and deeper walk with Him. Jesus emphasizes His desire for each individual person by using the words "you" or "your" eight times in this one verse. Jesus meant for this to be a very personal invitation into His presence. This is a very intentional statement made by Jesus. He wanted His followers to be able to use His words here as a very clear roadmap to a closer walk with the Father. This Scripture is an instruction manual telling us how we can have intimacy with the Father. We must find a place to pray, shut out the world, and *then* in that secret place, seek the Father. Jesus promises us that when we seek the father, He will already be there waiting on us. WOW! The Creator of the Universe wanted to give you clear details on how to have a personal, private and secret place prayer conversation with Him every single day.

When we dig in deeper we understand what Jesus was trying to tell us, Jesus wants us to get to know the Father. As we get to know the Father, He will reveal His heart and then we will learn how to pray the will and plans of God. When we find God in the secret place, He reveals our destiny to us. The more time we spend with Him, the more He reveals our destiny. When we start to walk in this type of intimacy with the Lord, we will understand the power and authority that we have as children of God. Jesus ends this statement in Matthew 6:6 by promising that when we seek God in secret, He will reward us openly. What is our reward? The reward is the explosive joy we experience as we fulfill our daily destiny with the Lord.

If we continue in the secret place with the Lord, we will start to grow closer and closer to Him. We will find out more and more each day who we are in Christ. As we continue to grow in our personal identity through intimacy with the Lord, our destiny will be unlocked at a greater measure every day. I encourage you every day to have a set time that you, just as this scripture says, go into your room, shut your door and seek the face of God the Father.

WALKING IN KINGDOM POWER

Devotion 2

Mark 1:35 "Now in the morning, having risen a long while before daylight, Jesus went out and departed to a solitary place; and there He prayed." (NKJV)

Many years ago, I was seeking the Lord in the secret place. I asked the Lord to give me one scripture that I could hang onto for the rest of my life. The Lord spoke "Mark 1:35" to me. At this time, I did not know this verse off the top of my head, so I went and looked it up. When I read it, I understood why the Lord spoke this particular verse to me. Very early in the morning, before the day had even begun, Jesus Christ would get up to seek the face of His Father. Before anybody got up and started asking Him questions or anyone was pulling on His anointing, He already had his daily time of devotion with God. He made an effort to get up and seek out a quiet spot away from everybody else so that it was just Him and God.

Jesus was very strategic in His prayer life. His prayer life was planned, it was private and it was personal. The word prayed in this scripture means continued action, not just for a brief moment. Jesus had a constant and continual prayer life where He drew strength from time spent with His Father. All throughout scripture we see that prayer was the primary tool that the powerful men and women in the Bible used to connect with God. It was through these times of prayer that these great people of faith heard the Lord and stepped out into the unknown to complete the destiny that He had placed on their life. When we hear a fresh word from God in our daily time with the Lord, it will send us out to make a difference in the geographical location that God has assigned us to that very day.

Each day, early in the morning when I spend my personal time with the Lord, I receive a fresh word that I will later impart to someone else. Seeking the Lord early in the morning gets our gaze upon the Lord and our mindset clear for the day in front of us. No matter what may come your way if you have been with God, you will walk in destiny. Seek the Lord early and allow Him to reveal more of your destiny to you daily.

WALKING IN KINGDOM POWER

Devotion 3

Isaiah 41:10, "Fear not, for I am with you; Be not dismayed, for I am your God. I will strengthen you; Yes, I will help you, I will uphold you with My righteous right hand."

This is one of the most powerful scriptures in the Bible about destiny. The Lord makes seven distinct remarks in this one verse. The first two words simply state, "Fear not." This should be enough for us but the Lord graciously continues to speak. Then He affirms us by letting us know that He is with us. How in the world can we ever consider not fulfilling our destiny when the Lord is telling us that He is with us? The third thing the Lord says is, "Be not dismayed." The word dismayed has 4 different definitions.

The first definition of dismayed is to consider. You cannot even consider for one moment that you will not fulfill your destiny and hit the mark where God has aimed you. The second thing dismayed means is to inspect. You can never inspect the possibilities of not completing the call and destiny that God has on your life. The third definition is to ponder. Never focus you on the illusion that you will not complete your destiny. The fourth definition is to gaze. Never gaze upon the negative or listen to critical voices. A negative mindset and negative people will pull you away from the destiny God has for you.

In the second part of this verse, the Lord again states, "For I am your God." Then God promises to strengthen us. I love the next part of this verse, God interrupts our silent thoughts and questions and says "Yes, I will help you." God is affirming His children once again that He will keep His promise to strengthen and help them. Then the Lord promises that it is His mighty hand on our lives that will hold us up. Friends, God Almighty has spoken to us through this scripture. He is assuring us that He is with us and because He is with us we have no reason to fear. With God by our side we will not fail as we pursue our God-given destiny.

I encourage you today not to fear! God will strengthen you and you will complete your daily destiny with Him every day. Remember, have no fear because the Holy Ghost is here!

WALKING IN KINGDOM POWER

Devotion 4

Galatians 6:4 "Let everyone be devoted to fulfill the work God has given them to do with excellence, and their joy will be in doing what's right and being themselves, and not in being affirmed by others." (TPT)

The happiest people that I have ever been around in my life are those who have found their God-given destiny and completely thrown their life into everything that God has planned for them. Every one of us has God-given gifts, talents and abilities. The Lord has given each and every one of us a wonderful destiny. The thing is we must find out what we are called to do and completely give our life to it.

This scripture encourages and teaches us that every one of us needs to devote our life to the work that God has given us. Never do it halfheartedly but do it all with excellence. By doing this, joy will spring forth out of our heart and flood our lives because we are doing what is right. The world needs to see real and genuine people being themselves and living lives that overflow with joy because they know they are in the middle of God's will. These people access new levels of their destiny daily by pursuing a personal and intimate relationship with Jesus Christ. When we consistently seek God, we are affirmed by the Holy Spirit on a daily basis. Therefore, we do not need affirmation from others to make us feel valuable. When the One who created the heavens and the earth affirms us daily in our secret place, we will be sure of our identity.

Each year, as I continue my daily walk with God, it seems that I find out a little bit more of who I am in God and what I'm called to do. It seems that in every season God is doing something new, wild, fresh and exciting. As my wife and I have been on this journey for numerous years together life gets better, sweeter and a lot more adventurous the longer we are together. We have completely given our lives to family, friends and ministry. We have fully embraced the journey God has laid out before us and taken every challenge and trial head on. My friends, I would not trade anything for where we are today and it all started in the secret place with God and growing daily in our destiny with Him.

WALKING IN KINGDOM POWER

Devotion 5

1 Timothy 4:14-15, "Do not neglect the gift that is in you, which was given to you by prophecy with the laying on of the hands of the eldership. Meditate on these things; give yourself entirely to them, that your progress may be evident to all." (NKJV)

Have you ever thought about how unique you are? I'm talking about your individual giftings, talents and abilities that God gave you. The reason that God gave you all of these specific abilities is for His purpose. So many people make a living off of their God-given talents but do they ever impact make an impact for kingdom of God with their gifts? 1 Timothy 4:14-15 is basically saying this, "Don't neglect the things that God has put inside of you. You also need to remember every single prophetic word that has been spoken over your life when men and women of God laid hands on you to impart into you. And also, you need to remember all of the words the Lord dropped straight into your spirit.

You have a great and wonderful destiny from God and He has given you every talent and ability that you need to accomplish your destiny. The Lord gave the body of Christ prophets and apostles to speak words over of encouragement and impartation. God's desire is to see you rise up and fulfill the destiny He has for you.

It is important for us to meditate on the things that will propel us into our God-given destiny. We must never meditate on the things that could hold us back from completing the call that God has for us. We must completely sink our life into our destiny. When you are running on all cylinders, your life will speak loudly of all the great things the Lord can do. People will see the process that you went through to get to the promise and every person who knows you will see the evidence of God's hand upon you. Your life will encourage them to give their life wholeheartedly to the God-given destiny that He has placed on their life. My friend, don't neglect the call or destiny God has placed on your life. Do not hold your gifts back from the Lord because He is the one who gave them to you. Allow God to do all that he has equipped and trained you to do in and through Him.

WALKING IN KINGDOM POWER

Devotion 6

Philippians 4:8, "Finally, brethren, whatever things are true, whatever things are noble, whatever things are just, whatever things are pure, whatever things are lovely, whatever things are of good report, if there is any virtue and if there is anything praiseworthy—meditate on these things." (NKJV)

How much more obtainable do you think your God-given destiny would be if Philippians 4:8 was your lifestyle. I want to challenge you to take a season of your life and do not allow yourself to think of anything negative about your God-given destiny. Don't try to talk yourself out of doing anything that God has placed in your heart. Do not focus on why something will not work. Do not look at the past when adventures or plans failed, instead look at the word of God and move forward.

What if in every situation and area of your life you lived by the truth of Philippians 4:8? What if you decided in every circumstance, situation and opportunity you would only focus on the things that were true, noble, just, pure, lovely, of good report and praiseworthy? How would this change your outlook on life? We can adopt

Truth *wnt*
1 *Trials*
2 *Testing*
3 *Temptations*

this mindset of always looking at the positive versus the negative. We must understand that everything that we go through truly makes us stronger. Every trial makes us wiser and more equipped to facilitate everything God destined us to accomplish.

The Bible said that King David encouraged himself daily. Each day, when I get up I go into my secret place of prayer and I encourage myself. I do not look to anybody to encourage me besides God Himself. Any other source of affirmation is just a bonus. When someone speaks something negative about me, I do not listen to it because I know the sound of my Father's voice. He has a purpose, plan and destiny for my life. My mindset comes from the truth in Philippians 4:8. I choose the good report over my life. I purpose in my heart that I will focus on the positive things versus the negative things. As for me and my house, we will live the Philippians 4:8 lifestyle. Choose today to change your mindset and daily allow yourself to get closer to the destiny that God has called you to.

WALKING IN KINGDOM POWER

Devotion 7

Matthew 7:7-8, "Ask, and it will be given to you; seek, and you will find; knock, and it will be opened to you. For everyone who asks receives, and he who seeks finds, and to him who knocks it will be opened." (NKJV)

Matthew 7:7-8 will move you forward into your destiny. This verse can be broken down into three parts. You will notice that the three parts start with each of these verbs: ask, seek and knock. Then each verb is followed up by a promise. The Lord loves movement. He delights when the children of God come toward Him in pursuit of His face. God loves when His children aggressively pursue His presence.

This verse starts off with the word ask, now if you put the first letter of the three verbs you also spell the word "ASK". This is all because God loves to communicate with His children. It all starts when we open up our mouths and speak from our heart to our loving Father. This verse is about pursuing the Lord, continually moving toward Him by asking, seeking and knocking. Many times we will find the door that God will open for us will not be opened until our hearts are ready to receive what is on the other side of the door. Many times we ask God, "Why haven't you opened up the door to my destiny?" The Lord will not allow the door to be opened until He knows you can handle the promotion that He wants to bring your way. When God drops a hint in about your destiny into your heart, we start asking because we know it will be given to us. However, it will not be given to us until due season. We seek God, because we know we will find Him. We knock because we know that God has promised that if we keep knocking, it will be opened in due season.

In verse seven, the words "ask, seek and knock" are written in the singular sense. But in verse eight the tense become plural: "asks, seeks and knocks". This means seeking God is a continual process. We must keep asking Him daily, as we seek Him daily, and keep knocking on the door daily. God knows the right time to open the door to your destiny. In due season, when He knows you are ready, He will open the door. It is the daily pursuit of God that will prepare and lead us into our destiny. Every time you ask, every time you seek and every time you knock, it you are closer to your God-given destiny.

WALKING IN KINGDOM POWER

Devotion 8

Matthew 16:9, "And I will give you the keys of the kingdom of heaven, and whatever you bind on earth will be bound in heaven, and whatever you loose on earth will be loosed in heaven." (NKJV)

This is a destiny scripture! Jesus says, "I will give you the keys to the kingdom of God." You have the power and authority to bind anything on earth. When we pray we have the power to bind any- wholism thing that is coming against us spiritually, physically, emotionally and financially. Anything that tries to stop us from getting to our prophetic destiny that God has spoken to our hearts. We have got the power to bind that thing up in the name of Jesus. Jesus also gave us the power to loose anything that is already bound up and needs to be free. We have to take our rightful position as sons and daughters of God and start walking in the authority God has given us. To walk fully in your destiny daily, start binding and loosing things on earth as they are in Heaven.

When God gives you a destiny, He will give you the keys of the Kingdom of heaven to unlock everything that you need on earth to accomplish it. Our destiny is a journey. As we embark on this journey, we must keep in mind the visual picture of having the keys of the Kingdom. Every time we come against a trial, tribulation or test we realize that we've got the keys in our hand to unlock or lock up anything we need to on your journey. In order to reach our God-given destiny, we must use the power and authority God has given us. There may be a resource that you need loosed in your life to help fund your ministry, business or family.

The power of life and death are in our tongues my friends. To exercise our authority, all we have to do is open up our mouths and speak to the mountain and it will be removed! We have the keys to the kingdom, and the power and authority from God to help us reach our destiny. So today, as you get ready to take on life, realize that you are already victorious. You are a child of the Most High God, walk in your authority and use the power of God to accomplish your daily destiny today!

WALKING IN KINGDOM POWER

Devotion 9

Philippians 4:6-7, "Be anxious for nothing, but in every-thing by prayer and supplication, with Thanksgiving, which requests be known to God. 7 and the peace of God, which surpasses all understanding, will guard your heart and mind through Christ Jesus." (NKJV)

To be a person of great destiny, we must fully understand the meaning of Philippians 4:6-7. Whatever God has destined for you, there is a process of development that God will take you through to prepare you for your destiny. God has perfect timing for every season of your life. To motivate you, He will show you the end result prophetically. But we must remember that the journey towards our destiny is just as important as the end result. This is why the Scripture states that we should be in prayer and supplication rather than being anxious for our destiny to mature. As we see the destiny unfolding right before our eyes, we get very excited. Our excitement can sometimes cause us to become anxious to see what the full fruition of what your dream will look like. We have seen a vision of our destiny in the supernatural and as it is unfolding before us as we go through the process. We walk through different seasons and take steps of obedience as God lays them before us. We should always remain thankful during the process because the process is what makes us strong enough to handle the final destination.

This is why the peace of God is so important. When we don't understand everything that's going on during our destiny journey, we can rely on the peace and the faithfulness of God. When our process is over and the specific season of our destiny at hand, God wants us to be full of His spirit with our hearts and minds in the right place. He doesn't need us to be worn out, tired or weary from the journey because and when our due season arrives. We will need to be full of energy and strength to accomplish all that God has placed in our hearts. Many people are so worn out by the end of the process that they cannot obtain the promise. My friends, it's our daily walk with God that gives us strength and carries us through to destiny. Stay strong, and enjoy the process because God is making you a champion for Him. If you stay on course, you will hit your mark and become all that God called you to be.

WALKING IN KINGDOM POWER

Devotion 10

Philippians 3:14, "I press toward the goal for the prize of the upward call of God in Christ Jesus." (NKJV)

To complete the call that God has placed upon your life, you must press into the Kingdom of God on a daily basis. I love how the Philippians 3:14 starts out with the personal pronoun I, which makes it very personal. The second word is the word press. Press means to move forward toward something. The word goal in this passage refers to a finish line at the end of a race. Many people are goal oriented and like to set goals. Just like guys in the gym that always ask each other, "How much can you bench press?" These guys are pressing towards a goal to become stronger. They mark their strength by how much they can lift or how much weight they can get under and successfully press it off. Bench pressing is natural strength but this passage is talking about supernatural strength.

Our prize is the upward call of God in Christ Jesus. The word upward in this passage is talking about a Heavenly calling. God has placed an upward call on every one of our lives. Through a close personal and intimate relationship with Him we will find out our

God-given destiny. We can't compare our destiny with anybody else's because we can't go to anyone but God to find out what our destiny is. We must find out what God has called us to do and then give our life to that.

We have to press in towards the Lord daily by seeking His face and getting to know Him more. As we spend time with God we will learn His characteristics. The closer we are to the Lord, the more we will know about ourselves because our true life is hidden in Christ. When you have a daily relationship with the Lord, pressing toward the mark He has for you will become easy. Think about it this way, if you are shooting a gun and you are not aiming towards a mark, you will just be shooting into the air. If you and your family left for a vacation without a final destination, you would be traveling aimlessly. My friends, as we draw close to God daily, we become closer to our destiny and become aimed at the mark God desires us to hit. Every day we press towards the goal that God has set before us by daily walking with Him.

WALKING IN KINGDOM POWER

Devotion 11

Proverbs 3:5-6, "Trust in the Lord with all your heart, and lean not on your own understanding; In all your ways acknowledge Him, and He shall direct your paths." (NKJV)

I want to dedicate this devotion to my mom & mother-in-law because this verse is their favorite scripture. Proverbs 3:5-6 are some of the most powerful and popular scriptures in the Bible. These life altering verses can be broken into four parts:

1. Trust in the Lord with all of your heart. When you see the word heart in scripture it is referring to two different parts of your being, your soul and your spirit. We understand that the Holy Spirit is the spirit that dwells within us, but our soul is made up of our mind, will and emotions. When our spirit rules over our soul, then our mind and emotions are properly aligned.

2. The reason it says, "Lean not unto your own understanding" is because many of us naturally overthink things or try to do what we think is right. As you are walking toward

your God-given destiny, you will step into things that you don't understand. But remember, God knows exactly where you are and will get you where you need to go. When we don't understand, we have the opportunity to allow God to truly father us. Times of uncertainty will teach you to lean into Father God and trust Him instead of yourself. This is why stepping out into the unknown is so exciting and challenging.

3. When we acknowledge God in all of our ways, in every single aspect of our life and do not allow the enemy any foothold, things will always work out. As we acknowledge God in every area, we become closer to our destiny in God.

4. The promise of these scriptures is that God will direct our path. When we set our heart, mind and gaze is upon Him, God will do what we could not do on our own or in our own understanding. As we put all our trust in Him, God will make a way where there is no way.

As children of great destiny, so many times we look at our abilities, talents and gifts and forget that God gave them to us. Never try to figure things out from a natural mindset. Instead trust and lean upon God for everything. Do not lean towards earthly but towards Godly wisdom. Whichever way you lean is the way your path will be directed. The Lord wants to direct our path but we must lean into Him and allow Him to lead us. As we daily lean into Him, God will lead us into destiny, because our destiny is only found in God.

WALKING IN KINGDOM POWER

Devotion 12

Genesis 1:26, "Then God said, "Let Us make man in Our image, according to Our likeness; let them have dominion..." *(NKJV)*

When God said to Jesus and the Holy Spirit let them, meaning people, have dominion, He meant we have dominion, rights and power. God has never lied nor will He ever lie. He states something one time and His word puts the rule into effect. He gave us dominion which means when God wants to do something on earth He is always looking for man or woman of God to establish His will and Kingdom into the earth through them. Therefore God is always working in us because God has a greater purpose to work through us. He will never give us more than our character and integrity can handle. That's one reason the Holy Spirit is constantly working us. He is working on us so that God can reveal greater realms of our destiny to us. When God wants to establish something on earth, He is always looking for a willing vessel whose heart is bent towards the things of God. Many people are limited by what they can do for God because they will not allow the Holy Spirit to do a greater work within them.

The Father, the Son and the Holy Spirit are always looking for someone they can plant a seed of destiny into. God has so many dreams that He wants to impart to His sons and daughters. There are more business ideas, ministry ideas, and entrepreneurial calls than you can imagine. All of these brilliant, Heavenly ideas are waiting to be downloaded into someone. There are worship songs that have not yet been written and messages no one's ever preached that will transform thousands and God is looking for someone He can trust to give these holy ideas to. You see when we are dead to the flesh and God does a great work through us, we always give Him all the glory. God has to cleanse us from self so He can work through us.

The more time I spend with God the more thankful I become for all that He has done in my life. I am thankful for every hard test, trial and tribulation I have gone through. Those are the things that made me who I am today in Him. If I never went through a hard time, I would not have realized how much I needed God to get me through. When I feel overwhelmed by anything, I know my God is faithful. I know this is true, if God gave me a dream, purpose, calling and destiny and my heart is 100% focused on Him, God will bring these things to pass.

WALKING IN KINGDOM POWER

Devotion 13

Jeremiah 33:3, "Call to Me, and I will answer you, and show you great and mighty things, which you do not know." (NKJV)

In this verse, Jeremiah is encouraging and urging the people to call out to the Lord. He is telling the people, "The Lord is waiting for you to call, and He is ready to answer." God isn't someone who is going to look at the caller ID and say, "No, I'm not going to answer that call." The Lord is eagerly waiting for you to call to Him because He already has the answer for you. Before you even pray, the Lord already knows what you have need of and He is already working on your behalf to bring your request to pass.

When we are closely walking with the Lord we find the destiny He has for us. When our heart is submitted to the Lord, He places His hope and dreams in our heart so we can carry out His desires. I pray, "Lord, put your destiny and dreams inside of me so I will carry out all the plans that you have for me." When we do this, my friends, we have all of heaven behind us.

The words call to me can be translated into "When you cry out to me". Throughout the Bible, whenever the words "call to" are written, it can also mean "cry out". God always immediately responds when His people cry out. Just like a parent if they hear their child call from another room in a calm voice, the parent will answer them but they will probably finish what they're doing then stroll into their room afterwards. Now if a child cries out, a loving mother or father would drop everything they have, stopped talking mid-sentence, and run or jump over the couch, dart around the table to get to their child ASAP. God is the same way. There will be times when you are on your way toward your destiny, and you hit a rough patch in life. Stop and call to the Lord, cry out to Him and He will answer you.

In the second part of Jeremiah 33:3, the Lord says, "I will show you great and mighty things which you do not know." This means God will do things for you that your natural mind cannot even fathom. Your natural imagination could not even draw out plans and ideas out as big as what God has planned for you! Every time I have called out to God and said, "Lord, I will do anything that you want me to do." The Lord has faithfully answered me, stretched me and challenged me beyond belief. While trusting in Him, I have been able to accomplish everything God has laid on my heart. God promised to show me great and mighty things and all they things God has shown me have been much bigger than I could have ever imagined myself doing. When God gives you a vision, He will always bring the provision and place people around you to make His dream and destiny for you a reality.

Every day we must daily call out to the Lord and make sure we are stepping closer each day toward our destiny. The application for this scripture is simple. If we call to Him daily God will answer us daily. He will constantly show us great and mighty things as our relationship keeps flowing with the Lord. Every day God still blows my mind as I live out the impossible with Him!

WALKING IN KINGDOM POWER

Devotion 14

1 Peter 5:10, "And after you have suffered a little while, the God of all grace, who has called you to his eternal glory in Christ, will himself restore, confirm, strengthen, and establish you." (ESV)

So on the road toward our God-given destiny not everything is going to be rainbows and roses. No friends, it's not. There will be trials and tests along the road but do not fear because God will always be there beside you. 1 Peter 5:10 says that suffering will come, but just for a little while. Don't worry because God has called you and given you a powerful destiny in Him.

When you go through something, the Word says He is going to restore you. You see when you go through something it makes you stronger. Every test and trial will teach you to lean upon the Lord instead of your natural strength. We cannot get through difficulty without Him. When you pass through a hard season, you will come out stronger in God. The word also says that God Himself will strengthen you. You must go through some things to strengthen you so that you will be strong enough to handle the destiny waiting for you at the end of your journey.

This scripture also says that God will establish you. We must always remember the journey is more important than the end result. You see the destiny is a combination of the journey and the vision God gave you to birth your destiny. The journey is what gets us closer to God. It is the daily moments with Him that pull us closer to Him. As we draw closer to the heart of Father God, He will restore, confirm, strengthen and establish us to keep going after our destiny. James 1:12 says, "Blessed is the man who remained steadfast under trial." (ESV) Even in trials, we must remain steadfast in the secret place of prayer daily with the Lord. Romans 12:12 says, "Rejoicing in hope, patient in tribulation, continuing steadfastly in prayer." (NKJV) In tribulation, we must be steadfast and refuse to be shaken out of the place of prayer. Our private time with God in prayer and reading of the Word is our refuge. Remember dear friends, your God is fighting for you. Exodus 14:14 says, "The Lord will fight for you, and you need only to be still. (NIV)

WALKING IN KINGDOM POWER

Devotion 15

Ephesians 6:10, "Now finally, my beloved ones, be supernaturally infused with strength through your life union with the Lord Jesus. Stand victorious with the force of his explosive power flowing in and through you." (TPT)

Do you understand how powerful you are? That's right! You are very powerful, in fact, you are a force to be reckoned with. Whenever you gave your life to Christ, you became a child of God. As a child of God, you have off the chart power and authority. The problem is a lot of people do not walk in this power and authority. Many children of God do not take the benefits that are freely offered to us. We are to be supernaturally infused in our daily life as the Holy Spirit strengthens us. As we read the Gospels, we see the power that Jesus had. Jesus demonstrated this authority and power from Heaven on the earth. Jesus said "We would do greater works than He did". You are powerful, my friends.

The way that we receive more power from God is we have to die to our flesh daily and empty ourselves of self. We are called to be carriers of God's great glory. In every situation, we are called to stand victorious. God wants to do an amazing work in us, so that He can do an amazing work through us. In our own rights, we can do absolutely nothing. We do not have the power within ourselves to perform miracles, signs or wonders. However, when we completely surrender our desires and will to the Father, He makes His limitless and measureless available to us.

As a child of God, who is being led and infused by the Spirit, you have the same power and authority as Jesus! Nothing standing in the way of our God-given destiny is a match for the explosive power flowing in and through us by the Holy Spirit. Whenever we allow the spirit of God to rule and reign in our life, then we are taking daily steps toward our destiny. Daily seeing yourself getting closer to all that God has promised you is very encouraging. Some of you may have given up on your hopes, dreams, relationships, family members and destiny. I'm telling you today, walk in the supernatural, explosive power of the Holy Spirit!

Watch God restore everything that seems to be broken. Speak the word of God and prophesy over every dead situation and watch it come back to life. Some of you may need to call your destiny into alignment with every prophetic word has been spoken over your life. You can help form your daily destiny by the words that come out of your mouth, speak life!

WALKING IN KINGDOM POWER

Devotion 16

Jeremiah 32:27, "Behold, I am the Lord, the God of all flesh. Is there anything too hard for Me?" (NKJV)

If you could do anything in the world for God, without worrying about who's going to help you or how it's going to be funded, what would you do? Have you ever got alone with God and said, "God if you are looking for somebody to live a dream through, do it through me"? My God dreams big & wild dreams! Numerous times in my life God has told me about the dreams and destiny that He has for me. Every time His dreams have been so big and wild that I have asked Him, "God are you sure you have the right person?" I've even looked around and asked, "God, are you sure you are speaking to me?" That's my God right there. God always chooses ordinary people that love Him to do crazy, impossible things for Him. God looked at Moses and said, "Moses, I know you stutter, and I know they don't like you in Egypt. But I need somebody to go get my people." God looked at Esther and said "Esther, I know you can't approach the king, but girl do it anyway." God looked at Noah and said, "Noah, I know it's never rained, people talk about you like you're crazy, but go out there and build the biggest boat ever called the arc."

So what destiny has God laid before you? What are you doing on a daily basis to help equip and train yourself to get to that God-given destiny? Did you know when God gives you a prophetic word that that word is so solid that you can stand on it? Jesus told Peter to simply come and step out on the water. Peter was in the boat in the middle of the storm. In the middle of a storm on the water, the safest natural place to be is in a boat. But Jesus told Peter to simply come. When God calls you to come stand by Him in a storm that is the safest supernatural place you can be. So Peter couldn't literally walk on water but he could walk on the words of Jesus. He stepped out of the perfectly good boat and walked on something stronger than the boat, the word of the Lord.

My friends, you need to step out of your boat of complacency and comfort zone and step out onto the words that God has spoken over your life! Start living the dreams that God has placed inside of you today! I'm talking about to the ones that dream about doing wild, crazy things for God but you are afraid. Being afraid of what your family and friends might say will keep you from stepping out into your destiny. They'll probably think you're crazy but it's time that you live your God-given destiny! Say this with me, it's time!

WALKING IN KINGDOM POWER

Devotion 17

Ephesians 3:19-20, "To know the love of Christ which passes knowledge; that you may be filled with all the fullness of God. Now to Him who is able to do exceedingly abundantly above all that we ask or think, according to the power that works in us." (NKJV)

Today I want you to be challenged and changed forever. We serve a God whose resources are measureless. We serve a God who has limitless provision. We serve a God who has a vision for your life that will overwhelm you with His love. Whenever you get a God-sized dream or destiny, it will overtake you. These are some words I like to use to describe the dreams and destiny God has for you: absurd, insane, outrageous, ridiculous, wild, crazy, enormous, gigantic, immeasurable, oversized, massive and God-sized, God-given dream & destiny. Remember God isn't looking for the most polished believer out there, He is looking for somebody with a willing heart that He can equip to carry out His dreams and destiny on earth as it is in Heaven.

God has made every one of so unique in our physical appearance, do you not think that He would make our spiritual nature much more complex and unique? The call that God has on our lives is so deeply embedded inside of us that no one can completely figure out what God has for us besides God. God has given you a destiny that is so unique that it has to be independent from everybody else. Your individual destiny will fit into a corporate setting but never allow anybody to tell you what you must do. See in a democracy, everybody has an opinion. But the Kingdom of God is not a democracy. God is the supreme leader and the Kingdom is a theocracy.

You, my friend, are very special and were created uniquely by God. The closer you get to God the more your destiny will begin to unravel. Not everyone who is currently with you will be able to take the journey toward your destiny with you. This is sad but true. When you are running on all cylinders for God, it will seem that there are more against you than are for you. But remember, God wants us to be filled with all of His fullness and He will do exceedingly, abundantly above all that we ask or think or pray, according to God's power that works in us. Make daily steps toward your supernatural destiny with God.

WALKING IN KINGDOM POWER

Devotion 18

Romans 11:29, "For the gifts and the calling of God are irrevocable." (NKJV)

God has never made a mistake, nor will He ever. When God gave you that gift or talent He had a purpose and a plan to use it for His glory. I don't care how many times you've denied the voice of God and did not step out into what He was calling you to. Your calling is still there. It doesn't matter if you or someone you know has back-slidden and been in that condition for 20 years. That calling is still there. I've seen people in their 60s and 70s pick up a call that they had from their 20s and take off with it like it was just given to them fresh from the Lord. God has obligated Himself to keep His word. God has never changed His mind about you, nor will He ever. God is the ultimate Father who believes in you more than you will ever know. Maybe your destiny seemed so great to you that it scared you. Fear will cause to back away from God and your destiny. But if you look into His loving eyes you will see He is calling you back to restore you so that you can answer the great calling He has on your life.

One translation says, "The gifts and calling of God are under full warranty." That's right, you have a lifetime warranty stamped over your head. It's never too late to start a new adventure with God. Some of you are doing a good work for the Lord right now, but you're not walking in your real destiny. You may be afraid to step out into the unknown but when you step out you will tap into a power that you never knew was available before. My wife quotes Karen Wheaton all the time and says, "You have no idea what is on the other side of your yes to God." The only reason God gave you those gifts and that calling was because He needed it fulfilled on the earth. What an honor it is for every believer to carry out the calling that God has strategically placed on their life.

Never allow a setback, your past, what others say about you, or past failures hold back you from walking in the fullness of God's destiny for your life. Ask God to show you a vision of where you will be in a few years and I guarantee that it will drive you to take daily steps toward your God-given destiny.

WALKING IN KINGDOM POWER

Devotion 19

2 Timothy 4:7, "I have fought the good fight, I have finished my race, I have kept the faith." (NKJV)

The apostle Paul is writing this Scripture at the end of his journey. What a powerful statement to make at the end of one's life. Paul is saying, "God I have stayed in the fight my whole life since my conversion. The race that you laid before me I have finished it completely. I never strayed and I never backslid. I finished my race." The way Paul kept his faith was by keeping a fresh walk with God daily. You complete your lifelong destiny one day at a time. Today is the day you can make a fresh declaration to God by resolving from this day on you will serve God with all of your heart!

As we study the life of Paul, we see the numerous attacks and setbacks that he went through. In spite of all of that he endured, he still carried out his God-given destiny. There's three things that we can pull from 2 Timothy 4:7. The first is that we must fight daily to keep our walk with God strong. No one else on earth can do what God has called you to do. If you do not complete the destiny that God has for you, your destiny will never be carried out in the earth.

Secondly, we must press into the Lord daily to finish our race. Paul was shipwrecked, placed in jail and stoned but kept moving forward to finish his race. He preached the gospel until he was put in prison. He still didn't quit when he was thrown in jail. He pulled out paper and a pen and started writing the Epistles. It did not matter what attacks came his way, Paul would find some way to advance the kingdom of God. Paul was always aggressively pursuing his destiny. The third thing is Paul kept his faith. The way that we keep our faith is having a daily time in the word of God and in prayer. We must keep our walk with God strong. We must surround ourselves with like-minded Christians, who are also destiny driven. We must pursue destiny like it all depends on us and pray about our destiny like it all depends on God. It is kind of like two wings of a bird, they both need to be moving at the same time to move forward.

WALKING IN KINGDOM POWER

Devotion 20

2 Timothy 1:6, "Therefore I remind you to stir up the gift of God which is in you by the laying on of hands." (NKJV)

One day, my grandmother gave me a dictionary and told me to look up some of my favorite words. This was an old school dictionary, not a new, trendy dictionary that waters definitions down. If you look at a dictionary written in the 1700 or 1800s, one thing you will find is so many words that we commonly use in the English language have God attached to them. It's amazing. For example, take the word "destiny." Destiny means invincible necessity. What does the word "invincible" mean? Invincible means incapable of being conquered, defeated, or subdued. If something is invincible it cannot be beaten. The word necessity means this: that it must happen. The destiny that God has placed in and on your life cannot be destroyed, because God purposed it, it must happen.

Everyone has been given a God-given destiny. Destiny is centered around our daily walk with God and implemented with our God-given gifts and talents. Each person discovers their destiny differently. Some people will be in the quietness of a private prayer time when the Lord speaks their calling to them. While others may see someone functioning in the field they feel called to and decide they want to do that for the rest of their life. Sometimes, you may just know what you're called to do and then a prophetic word comes by the laying on of hands of a person of God which confirms your calling.

Remember, this one thing: our number one priority is to worship the Lord with all of our heart, mind, soul and strength. It says eight times in the book of Leviticus, "Be holy because God is holy." Our destiny will be fulfilled out of the overflow of our daily, private time with God. If going to a service is your greatest encounter with God each week, you've missed it.

Your destiny is invincible. Nothing can stop it besides you. There is such a necessity to walk out the destiny on our lives. My friends, be encouraged today, just like every one of our fingerprints is uniquely different, so is the call of God upon each of our lives. Remember, with God, you are invincible.

WALKING IN KINGDOM POWER

Devotion 21

Proverbs 27:17, "As iron sharpens iron, so a man sharpens the countenance of his friend." (NKJV)

You've heard old sayings like, "You are who you run with." Or, "Show me your three best friends and I'll show you, you." Or even the old saying, "Birds of a feather flock together." There is a lot of truth in these sayings. The people that you hang out with the most are the ones that will shape and mold you into who you're going to become. The people that you spend the most time with will sharpen you or dull you spiritually, morally, physically and intellectually. So let me ask you a personal question. I want you to look at your God-given destiny, Now look at the three people that you hang out with the most. Are these people going to hinder or help you reach your destiny?

Countless times I have seen people of great purpose and destiny hang out with people that have no vision for their life. The people with great destiny generally always stoop down to the level of the people with no vision. The people with no purpose belittle and dull the person who has great vision for their life. The purposeless person will always try to pull you down to their level. I've seen countless times people who have a God-dream inside of them cut ties with people who are not pursuing their God-given dreams. As time goes by the people who are laying dormant never changed. But the people who cut the ties started flourishing. Instead of spending time with aimless people they began running with like-minded people who also wanted to do something great for God. Two or three key relationships can either propel or park you on your journey toward your destiny.

The company that we keep is either excelling us or holding us back. My wife, Autumn and I are both intentional about surrounding ourselves with people who have burning hot, fiery passion for Jesus Christ. We want to share our lives with people that want to accomplish something great. Make no room in your life for toxic people. I surround myself with people who love prayer meetings, revival services, and people who allow God to pull every ounce of destiny out of them. I love to be around people whose dreams and destiny are much bigger than their reality. I love to be around people who put no limits on God.

The reason you need to stay around people who love God and keep themselves sharp is because every one of us will get tired and weary. We all need people around us to sharpen us. Likewise, you need to be there for your friends to sharpen them when they're tired and weary. All of us need a group or company of people who has their gaze upon the Lord and are driven to complete their God-given destiny. Today, ask yourself this question, "Are the people you are hanging out with getting you closer or further away from your God given destiny?"

WALKING IN KINGDOM POWER

Devotion 22

Jeremiah 1:5, "Before I formed you in the womb I knew you, before you were born I sanctified you; I ordained you a prophet to the nations." (NKJV)

Jeremiah 1:5 tells us that before a person is even born, God Almighty puts a mighty calling and a powerful destiny upon their life. The sad thing is so many people feel unworthy of the calling that God has on their life. Jeremiah replied in verse six, "Lord I cannot speak, for I am just a youth." It's sad but he was telling the Lord, "You've got the wrong person. You're calling the wrong person to speak on Your behalf, God." This is the exact same thing that Moses said. But God will call the most unlikely people to be His mouthpiece.

When the prophet Samuel went to Jesse's house to anoint the next king of Israel, Jesse did not pick one of the good looking, strong sons of Jesse who were living in the house. Instead God picked David, the forgotten son who was out tending to the sheep. Sometimes in life, the place that you are currently at may not look like God could ever have a promotion planned for you. But my friends, when you stay faithful, your promotion is right around the corner. You might feel unworthy, but you're called by God to fulfill the destiny God has placed on your life.

The Lord told Jeremiah in Jeremiah 1:7, "'Don't say, 'I'm too young,' for you must go wherever I send you and say whatever I tell you." Basically the Lord told Jeremiah,

"Follow my instructions and everything is going to work out fine." Friends, if you listen to the guiding and leading of the Holy Spirit, everything is going to work out fine. When God makes plans He looks at every strategical part of that plan to make sure it's a success.

Before you were even formed in your mother's womb, God already had a plan and ordained you to be something very strategic and special to the geographical location He placed you in. When we understand how much the Father loves us, then we understand the great details that He goes through to give us the specific plans He has for our lives. So many people feel like they have been overlooked by man but you have never been overlooked by God. Your Father is about to breathe favor and blessing upon you and multiply your efforts because He has put a powerful destiny on your life.

WALKING IN KINGDOM POWER

Devotion 23

Jeremiah 18:4, "And the vessel that he made of clay was marred in the hands of the Potter; so he made it again into another vessel, as it seemed good to the potter to make."

Our God is in the restoration business. Just like in Jeremiah 18:4, the vessel had a little blemish or maybe a small crack, whatever it was; we know that something wasn't right. The potter did not throw this vessel away. He simply took it in His hands and began to reshape the vessel until it was ready to be used again. You see the whole time this vessel was on the potter's wheel, there was action going on because it was constant movement. Even though the wheel was moving the vessel was still in the hands of the potter. Many times you think you are at a standstill season but the pottery wheel of the Lord is moving fast and His hands are upon you. God is reshaping you for your next season.

A new day is coming and a now moment is near. You will enter your next season. Learn to rest during transitions because the only reason God restores something is because He wants to use it again. You see in the natural when people restore a house it is to rent or resell it. You will go through many seasons of your life. When one season comes to an end, there is usually a time of recalibration. Just because you may have went through a hard season, a painful loss, or a damaging blow never think that God is done with you. His calling is still upon your life and your destiny is still hanging in the balance.

My friends, this is where you get up, dust yourself off, and get yourself back up on that wheel and say, "Lord, finish the work that you started in me." Always remember God wants to work in you first so He can work through you later. Today's devotion is dedicated to the marred vessels. This is for the ones who are about to make a comeback and silence all of your critics. I dedicate this to everyone who thought they were down and out. You may just become the comeback kid to all those who doubted you. I encourage you today, go read over all of your old prophetic words, spend some extra time with the Lord, and dig a little deeper in the Word today. For tomorrow could very well be your new, now and next moment.

WALKING IN KINGDOM POWER

Devotion 24

Ephesians 3:20, "Now to Him who is able to [carry out His purpose and] do superabundantly more than all that we dare ask or think [infinitely beyond our greatest prayers, hopes, or dreams], according to His power that is at work within us."
(AMP)

We cannot even begin to fathom the enormity and capability of our God. Many times we limit the Lord because of our natural thinking. Any limits God has are the ones we put on Him. Ephesians 3:20 takes all the caps and limits off. This scripture states that God will fulfill His purpose in and through us. This verse reminds us of how gigantic the destiny God placed inside of us is. God will do superabundantly beyond anything that we dare to ask or think. Wait a minute, I was had a flashback of when I was in the second grade. "I double dog dare you." You remember those days. So friends, I triple dog dare you to ask God for everything that He has placed in your heart. I want you to realize that whatever you have asked for or imagined, God will do superabundantly above all the things that you have dreamed about and far greater.

Ephesians 3:20 promises God will do superabundantly beyond our greatest prayers. So what are you praying for? How much are you praying? The Word says everything that we pray for, that lines up with the will of God, will come to pass. Before you go to your next private prayer time say, "God, put in my heart and mind the things that I need to pray." Then your will becomes aligned with God's will and nothing is impossible. We don't ever want to pray out of the flesh. Instead always be led by the Spirit. Then Ephesians 3:20 promises God would do superabundantly above our greatest hopes. What are you hoping for? Never let your God-given hope die. God will not just bring the thing that you have hope for to pass, but He will do far greater than anything you are hoping for. God will do super abundantly above all that we dare to dream. My friends, you need to get a God-sized dream and dare to believe.

Right now, some of your dreams are starting to be resurrected. Things you thought they were dead are coming to life again. When God plants a dream inside of you it is like a seed. When God puts a seed in the ground is it planted or buried? If it's buried it will never come to life. But if your seed is planted, in the right season, it will produce fruit. Remember to ask, think, pray, hope and dream with God daily!

WALKING IN KINGDOM POWER

Devotion 25

Ephesians 3:19, "That you may come to know practically, through personal experience the love of Christ which far surpasses mere knowledge without experience, that you may be filled up throughout your being to all the fullness of God so that you may have the richest experience of God's presence in your lives, completely filled and flooded with God Himself." (AMP)

God has given you a personal invitation to get to know Him intimately. So many people know about God, but how many people really know God? So many people know about things but to really know something you must have practical experience. Ephesians 3:19 states that Christ wants you to know Him on a deeply personal level. You may have heard about the love of Christ all your life from family members, Sunday school teachers and preachers, but Jesus wants you to experience Him for yourself. The Lord wants your entire being to be filled with the fullness of God. When you walk in that fullness, you will have no room for the lust of the flesh or the things of this world.

God wants you to know Him by experiencing the richness of His presence. A lot of us have been in private or corporate prayer meetings or revival services where the presence of God was very strong. This verse tells us that God wants you to have the richest experience of His presence. When you have encountered something like this, nothing else in this world will ever satisfy you like the presence of God. God doesn't just want you to experience His presence, He wants to fill you with Himself. God desire you to be so full of His presence that you are flooded and overflowing with Him.

When we are completely filled and the Lord is still pouring out His power and presence over us, this means that there must be an overflow. Every person who comes in contact with us should experience the overflow of the presence of God. Your daily personal walk with God will overflow into your surroundings. Your family, workplace, hobby places, and everywhere you go will be changed the presence of God overflowing from your life. When we make daily steps towards God, we experience the richest measure of His presence and we overflow with everything that God has filled us with. When you know the One who has called you at a greater level, you will daily take steps toward your God-given destiny.

WALKING IN KINGDOM POWER

Devotion 26

Philippians 3:12, "I admit that I haven't yet acquired the absolute fullness that I'm pursuing, but I run with passion into his abundance so that I may reach the destiny that Jesus Christ has called me to fulfill and wants me to discover." (TPT)

Pursuing God is an amazing and fun journey. One reason for this is because no one has ever experienced the complete fullness of God. Because God is never ending and amazing, I can have daily encounters with the Lord every day that are more powerful than any revival service. In my daily pursuit of God, I am searching for one thing, Him. As I pursue Him, God reveals more of His destiny for me. I seek God more and more daily so I can know more about His personality and characteristics. When I do this, He responds to my seeking by telling me more about who I am and all that I'm called to do. When our true life is completely surrendered and hidden in the Lord, our daily pursuit is to seek him for who He is. These are those moments where He speaks to our heart and transforms everything. Our daily time with God shifts the atmosphere of our lives and brings new destiny upon us daily.

So many people are trying to figure out what they are called. Our ultimate purpose is to seek the face of God and worship Him with everything that we have. When we seek Him, it is His good pleasure to reveal our destiny and the great things that He has reserved for us. God wants you to discover your purpose because there is great reward for the Kingdom of God when you have laid your life down, completely surrendered to the call of God. The Lord is asking for us to recklessly abandon our hearts and minds. He wants us to forsake all of our selfish motives and simply say, "God, I want all that you have for my life. You have my yes Lord, and I will do what you've called me to do. I will go where you've called me to go." This type of surrendered and seeking lifestyle is what gets us closer to our daily destiny. The world needs to see real and genuine lovers of Jesus Christ fulfilling everything God has called them to do.

WALKING IN KINGDOM POWER

Devotion 27

James 4:7, "Therefore submit to God. Resist the devil and he will flee from you." (NKJV)

God has always longed for His people to have their heart completely submitted to Him. The Lord wants us to allow our roots to run deep wherever He has planted us. The enemy always tries to get us to be double minded and not let our roots run too deep. The enemy likes for us to always want to jump from one place to another and be wishy-washy. But God is looking for a man or woman who will submit to the destiny He has laid before them, and completely throw their life into the call that God has for them. When you completely surrender to the ways of the Lord, you will experience a greater dimension of the presence, power & authority of God. The enemy will always come at you but when you fully resist the devil, the Word says he will flee from you. Many times people will not fully resist the devil. It may not look like blatant sin but you may be compromising in a few areas or becoming complacent in a few spots. If the devil can I get you to backslide, he will delay your destiny. He will try to make you tired and weary. But the enemy's greatest trick is to keep you out of your daily personal time with God.

Whenever we back off from the things of God, the enemy will always have a string to pull or foothold he will try to ensnare you with. When we are fully committed and submitted to God, we purposely resist the devil and he flees from us. The devil never goes to war where there are no spoils. If the enemy sees that there is no open-door that he can enter in someone's life, he will try to go to through someone else.

Let me challenge you today, where are you on the journey toward your God-given destiny? Maybe today you need to make a fresh commitment to the Lord and apply your life to all that He has called you to. Maybe you need to verbally resist the devil, serve the enemy his eviction notice in all of your thoughts and actions. Today do whatever it takes to get back on the road toward your destiny. This is a new season for you! Start walking closer to God daily and you will reach your God-given destiny.

WALKING IN KINGDOM POWER

Devotion 28

Psalms 97:5, "The mountains melt like wax in the presence of the Lord..." (NKJV)

In this amazing journey, as we embark on the path of numerous God adventures, many times obstacles to try to stand in our way. Whenever you are pursuing your destiny you must always remember this one thing: take everything to God. When you find God, you receive His presence. Numerous times in my life, when there seemed to be a mountain in my way, I would always take it to the presence of the Lord. Then, in His presence, the mountain would literally melt away in my mind and I no longer saw the obstacle standing before me. Instead I saw the promises of God standing before me.

A mountain is something that would take so much of your time to walk around, or even to climb over. Climbing a mountain is not very safe but the presence of God is. Sometimes people feel like their promise is on the other side of a mountain and they must climb it to get to it. But in the presence of God, that obstacle will melt away before you. Instead of walking around the mountain or spending days climbing over the mountain, you can just walk right over it, as if it's a flat surface.

Another translation says hills instead of mountains. If you've ever seen hills, if they are all right next to each other, they go up and down up and down and up and down. The hills in your journey with God have to come into alignment with the prophetic words that God has spoken over your life. Every obstacle must bow its knee to the Lord and every attack of the enemy will fail. No hindrances in your life will be able to hold claim to you when you take it to the presence of God. In the presence of God, all truth is revealed by the Holy Spirit. God's presence is there to encourage you and Holy Spirit is there to speak to you. Your mountains and hills will melt away before you.

If you have obstacles holding you back from your God-given destiny, I encourage you to get into the presence of God, begin to worship the Lord, get into the word of God, and declare all of the prophetic words that God has spoken over your life. Start making steps again straight over that flattened mountain toward your God-given destiny.

WALKING IN KINGDOM POWER

Devotion 29

Psalms 91:1, "He who dwells in the secret place of the Most High shall abide under the shadow of the Almighty." (NKJV)

Psalm 91:1 gives me so much serenity. You should take a deep breath and a sigh of relief. Many times when God calls us to something, it can be a little overwhelming because the Lord never calls us to something that seems easy. He also does not call us to anything within our comfort zones. God sees how much potential we have inside of us and stretches us to pull our potential out. Psalm 91:1 states that you can dwell in the secret place of the most high. The word dwell means to live, set up establish, build, or reside. This verse is describing those that have made up their minds to live their entire lives in the presence of God, in that place of communion with the Lord. We know that secret place means the place of prayer, where it's just you and the Lord. Then Psalm 91:1 says that we can abide under the shadow of the Almighty. Abide means to live in or be found completely in something. This means we can daily dwell and abide in the presence of God.

When you're in the presence of God all of your worries, cares, fears, and doubts are taken away. If you removed every obstacle that is holding you back from aggressively pursuing your God-given destiny, you would have freedom to run after all that was in your heart. My friends, this scripture just gave you that invitation into a lifestyle of God's presence. When you build a strong dwelling place of prayer and daily communication with the Lord, you will truly be hidden under His shadow. Abiding in all of His power and love, you will be able to take daily steps toward your God-given destiny. Every day when we establish ourselves in the place of prayer with the Lord, we are setting ourselves up to advance the kingdom of God that day.

My friends, when you have an encounter with the Lord every day, everyone around you is going to be impacted by it. You will respond to situations different, act differently and talk differently because you are different. You will be living your life from the place of communion with the Spirit of God. When you are established in the secret place with God daily, you proceed with revelation from the Lord instead of natural wisdom. Your countenance will be one that has been with the Lord. The Lord speaks the deep things to the people who are found in His presence on a daily basis. These daily conversations with God will help unlock the mysteries that help you get closer to your God-given destiny on a daily basis.

WALKING IN KINGDOM POWER

Devotion 30

Matthew 6:33, "But seek first the kingdom of God and His righteousness, and all these things shall be added to you."
(NKJV)

Seek means to attempt to find something. Matthew 6:33 says the first thing that we are to seek is the kingdom of God and His righteousness. People of great destiny understand that they must give attention to the most important things, first thing in the morning. This is what Jesus did in Mark 1:35. Jesus sought out a solitary place to pray, first thing in the morning. Is the Lord your number one priority? Men and women of God who are full of the destiny of God, do not hit the snooze button. They spring out of bed ready for another God-filled day. There's numerous days, that I wake up way before the alarm clock goes off. I may be up two hours before the automatic timer on the coffee goes off because I know my God-given destiny. Every day, I seek first the kingdom of God.

How do I seek the Lord? In prayer, worship, reading the Word, and reading Christian literature early in the morning. Before the majority of the world gets up, I have spent my time with the Lord.

My mind is clear, my heart is full of the things of the Lord and I am ready to live out the destiny God has for me that day. My morning prayer time consists of seeking the face of God to know Him better and to read and study His word. I am constantly seeking to get a fresh prophetic word from Him in the morning. I do this because the second part of Matthew 6:33 says all these things shall be added to you after you have sought first the Kingdom. Jokingly, I say all the time, "all" in the Greek and Hebrew means all! All means everything! As a father, I love when my children want to spend time with me. When they come to me because they want or need something, I happily give it to them. But when they come to me just because they want to hang out and spend time with Daddy, those are my favorite moments of all. It makes my heart full and overflowing.

Many times we are caught up with the things of life and when we pray we just bring our lists of requests to God. We really don't seek Him or His kingdom. Then we wonder sometimes why things aren't happening in our life. When you seek first the kingdom of God, your heart will have a right motive and you will see the things of the Lord more clearly. When you seek first the Kingdom of God, you will see things the way Heaven sees them. It will change your perspective. Then you will start to make more progressive steps toward your God-given destiny.

WALKING IN KINGDOM POWER

Devotion 31

James 4:8, "Draw near to God and He will draw near to you."
(NKJV)

Complete freedom. This is my thought when I read James 4:8. I can see somebody walking towards God, and God loving, passionately, with powerful force and a huge smile on His face walking towards that person. When God walks toward you, everything that He is, is walking toward you. As you draw near to God, He is drawing near to you with His indescribable presence, power, provision, peace and freedom. When we have submitted our life to the Lord, we're like a seed planted in the most fertile ground imaginable. We are destined to succeed in everything that we put our hands to when we are led by the Lord.

As you wholeheartedly draw near to God, it becomes hard to do anything outside of the will of God. I love watching young children run with every ounce of energy they have towards their father. They are laughing and shouting and they don't care who is around them. They have no other desire but to get to their Dad. Then the dad usually bends down picks them up, hugs them tight and then lifts them up and tosses them up. This is how I see God reacting to each one of His children as they run towards Him in their daily walk with Him. As they read the Word, spend time in prayer, worship and seeking Him with all of their heart, He keeps coming closer and closer.

God has a breathtaking purpose and destiny for every single one of us. His plans are for us to advance the Kingdom of God and bring Heaven to Earth. Many times we will receive a vision or calling from the Lord and the size of this God-given destiny will scare us. That's a good thing. God will never give you a calling you can do by yourself. He is calling you into the family business, His family business. Your Heavenly Father wants to guide you, lead you, and partner with you in every single thing that you do. He's also going to finance your adventures. The closer that we draw near to God, we will be able to look into His eyes of love and see people the way that He sees them. We will be like John the Beloved who had his head on Christ's chest, hear the heartbeat of Jesus. We will have a heart for God's people like never before. Just like a child, when they're around their daddy, their fear and insecurities leave because they feel safe and loved. As you draw near to God, you are daily making steps towards the destiny that He has for you.

WALKING IN KINGDOM POWER

Devotion 32

1 John 4:18-19, "There is no fear in love; but perfect love casts out fear, because fear involves torment. But he who fears has not been made perfect in love. We love him because he first loved us." (NKJV)

Do you honestly realize how much God loves you? You don't have to answer that. Your actions truly do speak louder than words. One of the major reasons people do not completely embrace their destiny is because of fear. Many people say, "I think I know what I'm supposed to do" or" I feel I know what my calling is, but I'm not really for sure." When you know the Lord and He speaks to your heart, you will know what you're supposed to do.

Have you ever seen a little kid who is scared to ride their bike for the first time without training wheels? Or have you seen a child who is afraid to swing just a little bit higher on the swing set? The only way that child can overcome that fear is if their loving father reassures them. When a natural father is teaching his children these things, he isn't actually physically helping them one bit rather he is removing fear and telling them, "You're my child. You're going to be okay, Daddy's right here I got you." This is the same way God is with us. When God calls you to do something, He does it out of perfect love which means there should be no fear and no torment involved. Every step of destiny that you make, you will get closer to God and closer to the purpose He has for you.

Remember we have been made perfect in His love. God loves you so much and believes in you. The seed of destiny He put inside of you, he planted there by the Holy Spirit. He has every intention to bring that destiny dream of His to pass through you. Remember God has all the resources in Heaven and on earth to give you. If we can get a greater revelation of the Father's love, our fears and insecurities will be washed away by the love of God. As we daily seek the Lord, He will equip us in His love to complete the destiny that He placed in our hearts. So today, remember this: you are loved by the King and He called you to be a champion for Him.

WALKING IN KINGDOM POWER

Devotion 33

Acts 4:13, "Now when they saw the boldness of Peter and John, and perceived that they were uneducated and untrained men, they marveled. And they realized that they had been with Jesus." (NKJV)

Two ordinary men that had been in the presence of Jesus, head over heels in love with Him, became extraordinary. Now that's a sight right there. When people looked at Peter and John they could tell they have been with Jesus. These men were not trained up by a Rabbi, they had simply walked with Jesus. They were unqualified, unlikely men but they turned their life around and followed after Jesus. Therefore when people saw them they could tell that these men were marked and different because they had been with Jesus. Peter and John walked in the supernatural power of God. They walked by a blind man sitting by the side of the road that the religious leaders had walked by for years. But when two men who had been with Jesus passed by and grabbed his hand, this once crippled man was completely restored. People marveled because the religious leaders and the rabbis had walked by this man and he was never healed. But Peter and John had been with Jesus.

Have you been with Jesus? When people look at you can they tell that you have been in that secret place of prayer? Do you have fresh manna coming out of your heart and mouth? Have you been diving into the Word of God? When we make daily steps towards the Lord, our lives will unfold and reveal to everyone around us that we have been with Jesus. It doesn't matter what generation you're in, your ethnic background, your gender, denomination, education level, etc. What matters is have you been with Jesus. There is power and authority that God wants to release from Heaven upon the people that have been in the secret place seeking His face.

The countenances of Peter and John were just a little bit different from everybody else's. The way they carried themselves was different. The way they talked was a little bit different. They may not have the religious lingo or credentials of their day but they had the word of God in their mouths. They had the power of God flowing through their life. People marveled because they could tell they had been with Jesus. My friends, people need to marvel at our personal walks with God, not in our gifts, talents, and degrees. Our personal walk with God should make other people want to have that type of relationship with God.

WALKING IN KINGDOM POWER

Devotion 34

Acts 4:31, "And when they had prayed, the place where they were assembled together was shaken; and they were all filled with the Holy Spirit, and they spoke the word of God with boldness." (NKJV)

I absolutely love team ministry and the power of unity. When you get a team of like-minded people together, full of the power of the Holy Spirit, there is nothing in this world that can stop them. The two main words of Acts 4:31 are the words: they and all. It starts off and says "they prayed". This means the entire group, the whole crew, every person was praying, 100%. The Bible says where there is unity there is a commanded blessing. Then Acts 4:31 says "the place where they were was shaken." When you get a group of people together, praying in unity, that place will be shaken. That ministry, that business, that church, that home group, that outreach ministry, that marriage, that family you get the picture. Then it says they were all filled with the Holy Spirit. Who was filled? They all were filled, every last one of them. Then it says that "they spoke the word of God with boldness." It was not just one preacher who got up and spoke. No, they all spoke the word of God with boldness because there is strength in a group of people bond together in unity. Each and every one of them started walking in the love of God and sharing the gospel.

When you are part of a group of people, you may have an eclectic group with a lot of different talents, abilities and gift mixes. Each one of you will be able to share the word of God with boldness. You will have different occupations and different walks of life. When you surround yourself with like-minded people and you all pray together, you will shake the places that you are in and speak the word of God with boldness. My friends, when you are around a radical group of people who want to be flowing with the Holy Spirit, your destiny has a greater chance of survival. God intended for believers to be there to encourage one another and help strengthen each other along the way. The destiny that God has for each of us individually will also fit into a corporate group, just like many puzzle pieces come together to make one picture. Remember to do your part, to pray and walk in unity, and help shake every place that you're in. Your destiny is not just for you but it helps every person that you come in contact with.

WALKING IN KINGDOM POWER

Devotion 35

Ecclesiastes 10:10, "If the ax dull, and one does not sharpen the edge, then he must use more strength; but wisdom brings success." (NKJV)

I love the old story about the day the young, muscular, rookie logger challenged the seasoned, wise veteran logger to a challenge. The young rookie challenged the veteran to see who could chop down the most trees from sunup to sundown. The whole town anticipated this contest. When they started, they both started swinging their ax with strong precise strokes. As the day went on, the young rookie noticed the older veteran stopping to take a lot of breaks. He kind of felt sorry for the older veteran because he challenged the older man in front of the city for fun but also to prove he was the best. When the day was over, the young, rookie logger apologized to the older veteran and said, "I'm sorry I challenged you and embarrassed you in front of all these people." The veteran logger said, "You didn't embarrass me." The young logger said, "But sir, you must have been tired because you kept stopping to take many breaks. As you probably noticed, I'm young and I never stopped to take any breaks." The wise, veteran logger said, "Son, I never stopped to take a break. I was just sharpening my ax." After the trees were counted the wise veteran logger had cut down twice as many trees as the young rookie.

To complete the call and destiny that God has on your life you must to learn to stop and sharpen yourself. Whenever you see yourself getting dull, you can try to press through like the young logger did but you will not be effective. Instead, take the time, stop and sharpen yourself. Then get back to what God has called you to. You must know when it's time to keep pressing forward and when it's time to rest. There will be times that you need to go on a fast and spend extra time in prayer. There will be times when you need to stop and sharpen your personal walk with the Lord. Whenever I since myself growing dull, I generally go on a fast and intentionally seek God more. Taking the time to have a fresh encounter with the Lord will keep you sharp. My friends, we are going to hit our mark if we are in this journey of destiny for the long haul. Sometimes, the best thing you can do is stop and allow God to refresh and encourage you. Press into God, trust the process and take daily steps toward your destiny.

WALKING IN KINGDOM POWER

Devotion 36

Isaiah 42:9, "Behold, the former things have come to pass, and the new things I declare; before they spring forth I will tell you of them." (NKJV)

To complete the destiny that God has on your life, you must allow the past to stay in the past. You can't think about past circumstances. You must forgive people who hurt you and when you were overlooked and let it all go. You must set your gaze upon God and the future that He has for you. The third word in Isaiah 42:9 is the word former. Former has 3 similar meanings that I want to share with you.

The first definition of former means most. The former things of our life are the ones that we generally tend to think about the most. People who dwell on the things of the past usually deal with oppression and depression. They are generally negative people who are always talking about the past because that's where they live. When you see somebody who is negative and frustrated because of the past, that person's future is looking pretty dull. If you do not look where you are going you will have an accident.

The second definition of former means highest. The highest thing on some people's priority is worrying about the former things in their life. These people do not give much thought to the amazing, breathtaking purpose and destiny that God has laid out before them. Instead they hold the former things in the highest places in their minds.

The third meaning of the word former is past. These are all of the things behind us, but we cannot focus on them because our future is laid out before us. Then Isaiah 42:9 says, "The new things I declare." (Insert praise break) The past is gone and the new is in front of you, my friends. The Lord declares to you this day that they are new things about to spring forth. God has told you through a vision or prophetic word what your future has in store. Now choose this day what you're going to put your mind and your focus on. Will you focus on your amazing destiny that is standing before you or your past hurts, failures and disappointments? I choose to always look ahead to what God has in front of me. God will use your past as building blocks to get you where you need to go but don't go back, move forward. Aggressively make daily steps toward your God-given destiny. Lord, show us the new things that you have for us!

WALKING IN KINGDOM POWER

Devotion 37

Jeremiah 29:11, "For I know the thoughts that I think toward you, says the Lord, thoughts of peace and not of evil, to give you a future and a hope." (NKJV)

There's nothing more reassuring to a child than the strong, powerful confirming words of a loving father. How much greater is this verse to us because it was spoken by God the Father? I love the first part of Jeremiah 29:11 because God starts off by saying, "For I know" which lets us know right off the bat that God is saying, "This one thing, I'm telling you, I know for sure. Then He says, "I know the thoughts that I have toward you." This lets us know that our loving, Heavenly Father's mind is upon us. This scripture should bring so much confidence to us as sons and daughters of the Most High God.

God goes onto promise that the thoughts He has about us are good and not bad. This should break all illegitimacy off of us. The Father is thinking good things about us. We are in right standing with Father God which means we should stand up strong, with our heads held high, knowing we are His children constantly on the Father's mind.

In the last part of this scripture, God says, "I have plans to give you an amazing future." His thoughts for you are to personally give you hope that will make you hopeful about your future with God. This Scripture is letting us know that God the Father loves us so much that He sent His Son, Jesus, to this earth to deliver us and then sent the Holy Spirit to be our Comforter. God gave us the best He can give us two times: His Son, Jesus and His Holy Spirit. The Holy Spirit is working with us, to guide, lead us and be our comforter and Jesus is currently at the right hand of the Father interceding on our behalf. Jeremiah 29:11 lets us know that God's mind is upon us.

My friends, rest assured, knowing that all of Heaven is focused upon every one of us and their thoughts are upon us. God's thoughts about us are good thoughts to give us hope and a beautiful future. As the Word says, "We should go daily to the throne room and visit our Heavenly Father with boldness." I encourage you today, make aggressive steps toward your God-given destiny because your Father is cheering you on.

WALKING IN KINGDOM POWER

Devotion 38

1 Samuel 14:7, "So his armor bearer said to him" Whatever is in your heart. Go then; here I am with you, according to your heart." (NKJV)

We all need a few wild and crazy Godly friends. The ones that are just down for whatever as long it's aligned with the will of God. You've got to have some Holy Ghost ride or die friends. 1 Samuel 14:7 has two very important people in it. The first one is Jonathan who had a destiny dream in his heart. The second one is the young man who bore his armor, and encouraged him and said, "Let's do it." When God has called you to do something great for Him in the supernatural, it will seem that everything in the natural is stacked against you. But overcoming the odds is what makes victory so sweet.

Jonathan had a dream in his heart to go attack the Philistines who were trying to oppress God's people. There are times in your life when God is going to ask you to make a stand for something and come against the very things that are oppressing His people. There is greatness inside of you. God has placed powerful destiny and opportunities before you. You must find the right people to verbalize your concerns to. Find your ride or die Holy Ghost friends and then go after the things God has called you to.

Now some times we are called to be the young man in this Scripture. There will be seasons where we will need to tell leaders in our lives, "I've got your back. Go do all that is in your heart." Some of my greatest joys in ministry have been when I was helping spiritual mentors in my life do something that was in their heart. I put forth a lot of time, energy, finances and effort into seeing their dreams come to pass. God puts inside of us great satisfaction and rewards us when we help someone else complete the call and destiny that God has for them. I'm always encouraging the people around me to start that business, start that ministry, write that book, start the blog that is in your heart, and the list goes on and on. I want to be an encourager all the days of my life. Today may be the day you step out of complacency and normality and go after all the things that God has placed in your heart. So today start taking those steps toward your God-given destiny.

WALKING IN KINGDOM POWER

Devotion 39

Galatians 6:4-5, "But let each one examine his own work, and then he will rejoice in himself alone, and not in another. For each one shall bear his own load." (NKJV)

There will come a point in every one of our lives that we have to do a self-examination of all that God has called us to do. By doing this, we will have to look at every weak area and allow God to make us strong in those areas. We can't expect anyone else to carry out the purpose that the Lord has given us. Each one of us has our own unique destiny that each of us must accomplish. There are many gifted people afraid to launch out and do what God has called them to do. They will help other people accomplish what they're called to do, which is good, but when their time to launch comes they fail to step out. Look deep into your heart and see if there is anything holding you back from accomplishing the destiny God has laid before you. Then, take action on those insecurities and overcome the weak areas in your life.

Each of us needs to take the call and purposes of God for our own lives and take responsibility for them. If you could see all the things that God has laid out before you, it would probably blow your mind. God has so many adventures, plans, journeys, mountaintop experiences and excitement just waiting for you. If you can learn to live wild and free for God, your life would change radically. First, you must take responsibility.

We must all look at the life that God has given us and find out what He has called us to. Then we must press into Him, trust the process, and take responsibility for own life. In the Passion Translation Galatians 6:4-5 says, "Every believer is ultimately responsible for his or her own conscience." Many people are afraid to look at their destiny in the face and say, "Through God I will accomplish you." Therefore, they never fully carry the load God has called them to carry. They never take full responsibility of what God has placed on their life. Many people do not think they can accomplish all that the Lord has for them because they've never fully embraced the full revelation of sonship in the kingdom of God.

WALKING IN KINGDOM POWER

Devotion 40

Psalms 105:3-5, "Glory in His holy name, let the hearts of those rejoice who seek the Lord, seek the Lord hand his strength; seek his face ever more. Remember His marvelous works which He has done." (NKJV)

You will never accomplish the destiny that God has laid before you without giving glory to His holy name. Anything that we accomplish is because of what God did in us and through us. This is why we rejoice because without God, nothing that we do could be possible. Also, how freeing is it to know that nothing depends on us? God gave us the abilities and the talents to accomplish His will and then the wind of the Holy Spirit moves us forward to accomplish those. This is why those that seek the Lord will rejoice knowing that He is always with them. He is truly our strength, protector, provision, and dearest friend. This is the reason that we seek His face. All the glory goes to God!

Whenever you are going through a difficult time, just think back to all of the marvelous things that God has done. Look back at your prayer journals, when you were up against the wall and the

Lord made a way where there was no way. Remember when God healed you? When you received breakthrough or when those extra finances just showed up? Remember all the times God provided something at that perfect right moment. Our God is the perfect Father and we rejoice as we seek His face because He has us close to His heart and His benefits are always available to us. When you are fully committed and submitted to the Lord, every day you have a purpose. We walk in constant relationship and communication with him on a daily basis and our joy fully comes from the Lord.

The Lord has proven Himself faithful to me time and time again. He has come through with a countless number of healings, financial miracles, and breakthroughs at the right moments. I'm talking personally about my life, but how about yours? Reflect upon all the great things God has done for you in the past. Let that thrust you forward to know that if He brought you this far, He will make sure you complete the destiny that He has before you. Lord, we lean upon Your ways, and ask You to guide our daily life as we fulfill the destiny that You have for us.

WALKING IN KINGDOM POWER

Devotion 41

Galatians 5:16-17, "As you yield freely and fully to the dynamic life in power of the Holy Spirit, you will abandon the craving of this self-life. For your self-life craves the things that offend the Holy Spirit and hinder him from living freely within you." (TPT)

Just like the old song says, "Trust & obey, for there's no other way", many people are frustrated with their life. They are praying for the Lord to get them out of situations, help move mountains, or make things happen for them. But the truth is, they haven't completely yielded their life to the Holy Spirit. The Word says that as we completely, freely yield our own thoughts and opinions to the Lord. When we fully commit and submit our lives to the purposes and plans of God, then we will experience the dynamic power of the Holy Spirit working through us. We all think that we have a plan or strategy for life, but when we invite the Holy Spirit in at a greater dimension, He changes things.

Many times, you are the only thing holding you back from walking in your destiny. When we try to please our flesh or do things that seem right in the natural, we miss the supernatural leading of the Holy Spirit. God's thoughts are higher than our thoughts and His plans are better than our plans. Why do so many people refuse to freely and fully yield their lives to the guidance and leading of the Holy Spirit? There are certain things people do to offend or hinder the Holy Spirit. Nothing in our lives should hinder the Spirit of God. We shouldn't desire anything that holds us back from having closer communication with God the

Father. We should all want to walk in the full revelation of His love and blessings. Quit trying to figure everything out and learn to abide in all that God has for you!

We must crucify our flesh daily so we can live in a greater dimension in the Spirit. God wants us to walk in His fullness and to have the richest measure of His divine presence every day. As we daily take steps towards God, we are taking steps toward our destiny. Our true destiny is found in God. As we trust Him and submit to the process, we will complete our destiny.

WALKING IN KINGDOM POWER

Devotion 42

1 Timothy 4:12, "Let no one despise your youth, but be an example to the believers in word, in conduct, in love, in spirit, in faith, in purity." (NKJV)

Your spiritual authority is not reflected by your age, but rather by your spiritual character, integrity and wisdom that you have gleaned from God. I know many young people who have committed and submitted their walk to God and their lives reflect great favor and blessing. People will try to discourage you with their words because you are headed to a place that they haven't gone. Never let someone's controlling or critical words hold you back from your destiny because they're not willing to pay the price.

You got this! You can do it! Don't ever let anybody tell you that you can't do what God called you to do. People will try to shut you down because they don't think you can do God called you to. But remember, they are not God, and they didn't call you. They didn't walk with you through the valleys or fight your battles with you. So lift your head up, child of God, and don't listen to the negative voices around you. Never let anyone talk you out the calling God has given to you. God will take the least qualified person to prove He can use anyone because He is God.

Never let anybody tell you that you are too young, too old, too tall, too short, wrong denomination, wrong ethnic background, wrong generation or any other excuses. And the list goes on and on. You are the right person, at the right time, and you are about to do the right thing because God called you. When God's favor is on your life, all of Heaven is about to back you up with the provision and the wisdom of God. Your life should be an example to everyone. The faith that you have should make people marvel. The way that you live your life, the way you conduct yourself and the words that come out of your mouth should make people question their own hearts. Our hearts should always be pure towards God and man. Do what the Lord has called you to do and never let anyone speak an ounce of doubt over your God-given destiny. Listen to the words that your loving Father speaks over you on a daily basis. Use the encouraging words of your Heavenly Father to help you make daily steps toward your destiny.

WALKING IN KINGDOM POWER

Devotion 43

John 10:27, "My sheep hear my voice, and I know them, and they follow me." (NKJV)

Walking in the middle of God's perfect destiny for your life is one of the greatest feelings that you will ever know and peace will overwhelm your heart. Many people claim to be followers of Jesus, the good Shepherd. But are they really? Jesus said in John 10:47, His sheep hear His voice, and He knows them. When you know somebody you have communication with them. Jesus said that not only do His sheep hear Him but they follow Him as well. If you are a true disciple of Christ, you are one that follows after Him. Wherever His voice leads you, you will go. Many people claim to be believers, but they do not follow the leading of God's voice. The Lord is going to guide you and lead you through the voice of the Holy Spirit and true believers of God will always follow after His voice.

I love Psalms 23:1, which says, "The Lord is my shepherd, I shall not want." My favorite part of this verse is where it says, "I shall not want." We know that God's plan for us is good. His plan is to give us a future and a hope. We should be so content in the middle of the sound of God's voice over our life that we do not wander outside the leading of His voice. When we know God's goodness we will know that our daily provision comes from Him. Psalms 23:2 says, "He makes me to lie down in green pastures; He leads me beside the still water." God will always prepare a place for you. The green pastures represent fertile soil. God will always place you or plant you in the place where you can flourish. Sometimes it may seem like you're in a rough spot but you trust that you are growing because you are planted in fertile ground. The Lord will always put you by the still water. He will place you in a place where you can drink from the river of God that never runs dry.

Children of God hear His voice and obey His voice. Sons and daughters of God follow the leading of the Holy Spirit. Many believers will not follow the supernatural voice of God because they have to always make sure it makes sense in the natural. This is where we have to rely on the good Shepherd, knowing that He has our best interest in mind. We must trust that He will guide us and lead us to the right place. Following the Lord with all of our heart will allow us to make daily steps toward our destiny.

WALKING IN KINGDOM POWER

Devotion 44

James 1:22, "But be doers of the word, and not hearers only, deceiving yourselves." (NKJV)

Remember that time? That time you were reading the word of God and the Lord spoke to you prophetically about the destiny over your life. Or the time someone prophesied over you and it was exactly what the Lord had been speaking to you in your private time. Have you ever seen a certain occupation and said, "I could do that right there for the rest of my life"? So what are you doing with the word of God that is in your heart and all the prophetic words that have been spoken over you?

Many people go to church every Sunday, chase down revivals or their favorite speaker and never do anything for the Lord besides attend a service. The seed of destiny lying dormant in your life is about to come alive. This is your season, my friend. This is your time to become a doer of the word of God. It's time that you start living out the prophetic destiny that God Himself has spoken over your life that has been confirmed by the words of apostles and prophets. You were created for such a time as this to do everything that God placed on your heart to do. Now, no longer deceive yourself and try to talk yourself out of your destiny.

I want you to go back over all of your old prayer journals, prophetic journals and dream journals and ask the Lord to allow you to experience these words as if it was the very first time you heard them. Words from God have a transformational way of always being fresh and alive. Why is your favorite scripture, your favorite scripture? There is something inside of your spirit that goes off when you read certain scriptures in the word of God because they are directly linked to your destiny. When it's all said and done more may be said than done. Let that never be said about you, instead be a doer of the word of God. Never become satisfied watching somebody else do what they were called to do without fulfilling your destiny. Answer the call that the Lord has on your life and step into it today. Ask the Lord today to reveal to you the next step that you need to take toward your God-given destiny.

WALKING IN KINGDOM POWER

Devotion 45

Matthew 13:23, "But he who receives seed on good ground is he who hears the word and understands it, who indeed bears fruit and produces: some a hundredfold, some sixty, some thirty." (NKJV)

You are good ground. Now I want you to say that, say "I am good ground". You see so many times when God plants a seed of destiny in us it frightens us. Sometimes people think God picked the wrong person. God chose the right person, that destiny inside of you is the correct seed. You are good ground, my friend. The Bible says when you put the right seed into good ground you are about to see a harvest come forth. You may need to pray, "Lord, enlighten the my eyes of understanding so I will be able to understand the Word as it comes forth to water that seed that you have placed inside of me." This is the season that the seed that God has planted inside of you is going to spring forth and produce amazing fruit. John 12:24 point out that the shell of the wheat has to break open before the seed can produce fruit. The outer shell must break open and die so what is inside it may come out. You cannot be a natural thinker and go where God is about to take you supernaturally. You are about to be broken out of your comfort zone and completely out of complacency.

In this season, you will understand the things that God has spoken over your life. You will walk in greater revelation of why you were created. You will start to feel dormant seeds inside of you come to life and produce fruit. There is a harvest inside of you for the kingdom of God. As you spend extra time in the word of God and in the place of prayer, you will feel the seed that God placed inside of you being watered and nurtured as it starts to grow. There is kingdom fruit that the Lord is going to harvest through you. It may not have even broken through the surface yet. The world has not yet seen all that is inside of you but this is your now season. Expect everything God has promised to come to pass. Start making steps toward your God-given destiny and remember you are good ground that God has chosen to plant His great seed inside.

WALKING IN KINGDOM POWER

Devotion 46

John 3:34, "For He whom God has sent speaks the word of God, for God does not give the Spirit by measure." (NKJV)

When God sends someone He sends the full support of Heaven with them. We have to realize that there is no measure to God's great power and no limit to what the Holy Spirit can do through us. Many times, we limit God by our natural thinking. This should not be the case, my friends. You can and will do every single thing God has purposed you to do for Him and you will fulfill it to the fullest measure.

You see there is a battle for the seed that God has placed in your life. That seed of destiny can transform you, your family, your church, your city, your state, your nation and event the world! There are things inside of you that can redefine whatever occupation you do. Whatever business or industry you are in can be improved by the seed of destiny that is inside of you. This is why the enemy will fight you like he does but he won't be able to abort the seed of your God-given destiny.

The seed inside of you can literally change in transform your city. That seed will grow and produce Kingdom fruit. The enemy tries to cover your seeds of destiny with shame, guilt, condemnation, past failures, emotions, insecurities and father wounds. But God wants to heal you so He can transform you so you can transform everything around you. Jesus said the works that he did, we as the body of Christ will do greater. We must realize that we can tap into God's power and walk in the authority that He has given us. When God calls and sends you to something, He sends you with measureless, limitless power and authority.

You need to be around people who love you in seed form. Now, when you're producing fruit many people will like you. However, you need to be around people who will help train, equip and encourage you to be what God has called you to be. On the way to your destiny, remember that when you hit a delay, it is not a denial. You need to be around people who encourage you to keep going. You do not need people who will criticize you because you're not moving forward. The measureless limitless work of Jesus Christ is working in you, God has a kingdom purpose He has placed inside of your life and the Holy Spirit will lead and guide you into all truth. Walking with the Holy Spirit daily will help to make steps toward your destiny.

WALKING IN KINGDOM POWER

Devotion 47

Ephesians 1:18, "I pray that the light of God will illuminate the eyes of your imagination, flooding you with light, until you experience the full revelation of our great hope of glory." (TPT)

The more time you spend with God, the more He will open up your eyes to the great realm of possibilities that He brings to your life. The more we cultivate our relationship with God, the more our spiritual eyes are opened and we see the great possibilities He has for us. As we closer draw to God, we become like a tree planted by the river and we allow our roots to grow deeper and further into the things of God. Becoming deeply rooted makes us more stable, able to withstand strong storms, and allows us to produce more fruit.

There are 4 different types of people. I call these the 4 W's.

1. Watchers - They sit around and watch everybody else do something for God and get blessed as they watch and see what God is doing. These are the people that do a lot

of talking but not a lot of doing. They never act on what they say.

2. Waiters - This groups likes to sit around and wait and see what is going to happen. Then when things are great, they like to jump in but they never really have a role in what's going on. These people just come to roll with the flow but never have a say in anything. Waiters need to quit being so passive and become more aggressive.

3. Wishers - This is a pretty good group of people because they are positive thinkers. Wishers have really good attitudes. They really wish that God would do something awesome. Many times the Wishers have a lot of vision but they want somebody else to do it. This group is one step away of their destiny.

4. Workers – Workers are the group of people who are ready to roll up their sleeves and get their hands dirty for the kingdom of God. Workers are the people that are ready to fulfill their God-given destiny. These people will also help you accomplish your destiny. While the other groups are watching, waiting or wishing something would happen, the Workers are the movers in the shakers. They get a word from God and they attack it like a pit bull. Workers have hard working mentality.

Allow God to completely flood you with this revelation. Allow the vision that God has for your life to go so deep into your spiritual DNA that you will receive the great hope that He has for you. Allow God to put the seed of His destiny deep into your heart and let it drive you to make daily steps toward your destiny.

WALKING IN KINGDOM POWER

Devotion 48

2 Timothy 1:7, "For God has not given us the Spirit of Fear, but of power and of love and a sound mind." (NKJV)

When I read 2 Timothy 1:7, it makes me think of the old saying, "My daddy can whip your daddy." I think of our loving Father who has given us all power, authority and complete peace. So why would we allow anything to stop us from fulfilling the destiny that our Heavenly father has given us? I'm going to give you The 5 P's of Father God.

Protector - My God is the great protector of His children. Our father is the strongest force in the entire universe because He created. God will protect us from any and every attack that comes our way that may try to stop us from fulfilling our God-given destiny.

Provider - My God is the great provider. He provides us with every earthly and heavenly blessing we could possibly imagine. God fills us full of His Spirit and gives us godly wisdom and peace to His children. He makes a way financially for us to provide for our families. Holy Spirit provides great counsel by guiding us and leading us in our daily lives.

Promoter - My God is the great promoter. Whenever you need a job, He'll drop your name in the board room. When you need a physical healing, He dispatches healing angels to you. A true father always looks to open doors for his children and my God is the greatest Father there is!

Priest - My God is the High Priest. He is the high priest of your life and your family. Our heavenly Father is approachable. His wisdom and knowledge is unmeasurable and any question we may have, our priest has the answer to it. God leads and guides us into all spiritual truth.

Prophet - My God is our prophet. God will always give you a word when you need a word. His words are always 100% accurate and on point. John 1:1 says, "In the beginning was the Word, and the Word was with God, and the Word was God." (NKJV) God will always speak to you out of the written word, and make it apply to your everyday life.

Our heavenly Father is the perfect dad. We really have the best Dad in the whole world. God is complete in every aspect of fatherhood.

WALKING IN KINGDOM POWER

Devotion 49

Matthew 5:6, "Blessed are those who hunger and thirst for righteousness, for they shall be filled." (NKJV)

Blessed & Filled! These are two things that I definitely want in my life. I want to be blessed by God and filled with everything that He has for me. If I hunger and thirst for the things of God and His righteousness, then to be blessed and filled is my promise and my portion. Have you ever noticed the people that have the favor and blessings of God all over them? These are the people that have a heart for the things of God. The people that when they pray, they say, "God, I just want more of You. I want Your characteristics. Help me with my integrity and character." These are the people that want to be righteous and blameless before God. Their heart is focused on the things of Heaven and their mind is filled with the purposes of God.

The Lord spoke to me once about the people I was supposed to run with in life. When the Lord showed me Matthew 5:6, it was as plain as day. I was going to run with people who were hungry and thirsty for the things of God. The Bible clearly says that you will be blessed and filled if you seek Him and remain hungry and thirsty for Him. When you run with people who are hungry and thirsty for God and the things of God, they will add life and value to you. Why run with people who aren't blessed and who are filled with all that God has for them? If there are people that are trying to attach themselves to you who are not hungry and thirsty for God, they will never be filled with all God has for them. Part of their life will be empty and they will always try to find something to fill that empty void. Why live your life with people who will always have worldly things going on in their life?

Instead, find people who want to live their life wild and free for Jesus Christ. I want to run with people who are living recklessly abandoned to the thoughts of God and who have no care for the opinions of this world. These people will personally make daily steps towards their destiny as they are also helping and encouraging you to live your life to the fullest in God. My friends, if you want to live a blessed life filled with all that God has for you, remain hungry and thirsty for the things of Him.

WALKING IN KINGDOM POWER

Devotion 50

Matthew 11:28, "Come to Me, all you who labor and are heavy laden, and I will give you rest." (NKJV)

When we are not walking in the destiny that God has given us it is because we are doing so many things that man has given us instead. Life is busy but when we take on the cares and burdens that other people have placed on us, we carry unnecessary and heavy burdens. You need to spend a moment with the Lord and ask God you may have taken on that He did place on you. There is a huge difference between a Kingdom burden and the burden of man. Many times, we allow people to dump their burdens on us and we were never meant to carry them. We will be given the strength to carry the load that God has given us, not the load we take on ourselves. Supernatural grace comes in to help us carry what God has called us to carry.

The Lord is inviting us to come to Him, talk to Him and allow Him to speak to us. When we come to the Lord, open up our heart and express our thoughts and feelings to Him, then He removes the heavy burdens. This is how God gives you rest. He will speak His loving voice into your life and restore you. He will restore your vision, encourage you, and light your fire for Him again. When we spend that extra time with God, He removes all weights and heavy burdens from us. God will always give us rest from our earthly labor, and helps us to refocus on the call He has for us.

Psalms 85:6 says, "Will You not revive us again? That Your people may rejoice in You." Sometimes we need to stop and allow God to revive us again. When the children of God are tired and worn out, we are not a very effective witness. When we spend that time of fresh encounter with the Lord ,it sparks us and renews our relationship with Him. Our hearts are to rejoice in God. So ask the Lord, "Revive me again. Remove heavy weights and give me rest and strength for the next season of my life." God will answer you and help you refocus on your God-given destiny and make steps towards it.

WALKING IN KINGDOM POWER

Devotion 51

Ephesians 2:10, "For we are God's masterpiece. He has created us anew in Christ Jesus, so we can do the good things he planned for us long ago." (NLT)

Have you ever watched somebody paint a picture? While the artist was painting the picture, you may have thought, "What in the world are they doing?" You may have even tried to figure out what the picture was going to be. Nevertheless, the artist knew what they were making the whole time. While God the master craftsman, is working on our lives, we may not fully know what God is doing. The people around us surely do not know what He is doing but God has had a plan from the very beginning. When God starts a project, He has the end result in mind.

Sometimes you may not know why you are going through a certain test or trial but you can rest easy knowing that God will use it to your advantage. You may be in a situation right now with circumstances that you don't know how to deal with. Trust God and allow the Holy Spirit to guide you and lead you through this situation. During these times, understand this is part of the process that will take you to the promise. Whatever you may be facing is just part of the path that will lead you to your destination.

God has uniquely gifted every single one of us and never, not even for one moment, think that God has forgotten about you. He has not misplaced or punishing you. The Holy Spirit is guiding you through life, which may seem like an obstacle course at sometimes, but you're going to make it through just fine. Proverbs 19:21 says, "Many are the plans in a person's heart, but it is the Lord's purpose that prevails." (NIV) Sometimes we may think that we know exactly what we want and how things turn out. We may think we know what should happen but God knows what should happen. The Lord has an amazing way of always making His purpose come to pass. Sometimes it even seems when we have messed things up or circumstances have messed things, all mighty powerful God still has of way of getting us to where He needs us to be.

God has a purpose and a plan for every one of us. You are in the hands of the Master Builder and God is completing you for the purpose that you were created for before the beginning of time. Enjoy the process, my friends, and daily allow God to take steps toward your destiny with Him.

WALKING IN KINGDOM POWER

Devotion 52

John 14:12, "Most assuredly, I say to you, he who believes in Me, the works that I do he will do also; and greater works than these he will do, because I go to My Father." (NKJV)

Smith Wigglesworth said, "Only believe". For the children of God who believe wholeheartedly in Jesus Christ will live out the impossible and miraculous things of God. Our portion is to frequently see signs, wonders and miracles. Jesus stressed the point by saying "Most assuredly I tell you, that if you believe in Me, you won't just do what I'm doing but you will do far greater." You see the disciples were totally amazed at the power and authority that Jesus had and operated in. So one day He told them, "If you think this is awesome, you should see what the power I want to leave to you can do. You guys will do far greater things than I ever did." Many people can't fathom or understand that when Jesus went to be with the Father, He sent the Holy Spirit to us. We have to learn how to walk and operate in the power of the Holy Spirit.

Jesus was a great example as He ministered with regular signs, wonders and miracles. Jesus healed the sick, raised the dead, replaced severed ears, turned water to wine, walked on the water and performed countless other miracles! We must understand that we are placed on earth for such a time as this with powerful destiny placed inside of us. The children of God should be encouraged as we read the Gospels and the book of Acts, we have the same power that was demonstrated by Jesus, the disciples and the apostles! When we read books of great men and women of God that have gone before us, we should be encouraged knowing that we have got the same power available to us. There is nothing in this world that can stop you from completing the God-given destiny that God has on your life. No matter what trial or test comes before you today, you will overcome by the power of God!

Colossians 3:3 says, "Your crucifixion with Christ has severed the ties to this life, and now your true life is hidden away in God as you live within the Anointed One." (TPT) Our new life is completely hidden in Christ and our destiny is given to us by Christ. Therefore we rely on His power and revelation for things to happen. When we learn to completely rest in the voice of God, knowing that all provision comes from it, we cut off the old, and our mindset becomes that with God we can accomplish anything. Now you can rest easy knowing that as long as your true life is hidden in God and remain obedient to His will, you will complete the call and God-given destiny upon your life.

WALKING IN KINGDOM POWER

Devotion 53

Psalms 37:4-5, "Delight yourself also in the Lord, And He shall give you the desires of your heart. Commit your way to the Lord, Trust also in Him, And He shall bring it to pass." *(NKJV)*

I'm so thankful that our heavenly Father is so relational. Psalm 37:4-5 fills me with peace and thankfulness. It seems as if the writer is speaking with great excitement and joy through personal experience of the Lord's faithfulness. If we fully give ourselves to the Lord and delight ourselves in Him, then He will give us the desires of our heart.

I love that when we fully and freely commit our hearts to God, then we take on His likeness. Our hearts are filled with all of the things in the heart of God when we trust and delight in Him. Therefore when we do something out of our heart it is really from the heart of Father God. This is when we begin doing the Father's business. When our consecration to the Lord is strong and our relationship with Him is powerful, it's like two people dancing together perfectly. There are two but in reality they are one. I pray this daily, "Lord, I want Your desires to be in my heart so I carry out Your plans."

When we completely commit our ways to God and fully trust in Him, His Word and His heart will fulfill His promises to us. The Word of God is our guarantee that when we allow our lives to be deeply rooted in the place God has planted us; we will produce fruit for the kingdom of God.

Many people are trying to carry out the works of God but there countenance is poor because there is no delight in their hearts. Our God is relational and He will lay a life full of adventure, purpose, dreams and destiny before you. God is looking for people who will take Him by the hand and allow Him to lead them into so many adventures, along the path less traveled. Sometimes you have to make a path with God because you're going somewhere new and opening new doors for the people who will come after you. Every step you take with God is one step closer to your destiny.

WALKING IN KINGDOM POWER

Devotion 54

John 10:10, "The thief does not come except to steal, and to kill, and to destroy. I have come that they may have life, and that they may have it more abundantly." (NKJV)

A shepherd always comes on the scene to protect life, while a thief always comes to take life. The devil is always going to try to steal your destiny. The enemy will try to steal your dreams, your health, your friends, your family, your emotions and anything he can to try to kill God-given destiny. The enemy will do anything he can to try to kill your purpose, your motivation, your friendships, and your finances. The enemy will try to destroy you, in any way he possibly can. The enemy would love to destroy your name, your ministry, your family, your church, and your city. The thief has one purpose and that is to steal kill and destroy everything that God is trying to build.

But my friends, let me tell you about our God. He doesn't just come to give you life, but He comes to give you life more abundantly. He has a good plan and a great purpose for you. He has more provision than you could possibly imagine. He has more people to come alongside you to help you with your God-given destiny than you could ever need. My God is the God of more than enough. He wants to fill you with joy and peace. God's desire is to fill your heart and mind full of knowledge, wisdom and understanding. That's my God!

Many times the devil will try to steal, kill or destroy something but when God comes on the scene He will restore everything. He will give you sevenfold in return for every single thing the enemy destroyed. My father will bring double for your trouble. When the enemy steals something from you, you say may just need to tell the enemy, "I'm going to tell my Dad!" And when Daddy God comes, He's bringing a whole host of angels with Him. The enemy tried to kill me many times but through God I came back stronger. There were times the enemy used people to try to destroy me but I came back wiser. When the devil attacks you, he makes a big mistake because God will always bring you back better. The enemy needs to learn to quit messing with us because we are children of the Most High God. We are so full of destiny and purpose and the devil cannot stop the plan of God. Keep stepping toward your God-given destiny and when the enemy comes back you tell him, "You mess with me and I'll come back stronger!"

WALKING IN KINGDOM POWER

Devotion 55

Philippians 4:8, "Finally, brethren, whatever things are true, whatever things are noble, whatever things are just, whatever things are pure, whatever things are lovely, whatever things are of good report, if there is any virtue and if there is anything praiseworthy—meditate on these things." (NKJV)

I really love being around positive people. I like talking to people who are positive thinkers who tend to focus on the good things that could happen instead of the bad. Powerful momentum can come from having a positive mindset. What if you take a chance and step out into your God-given destiny?

People who take chances in life and take the opportunities that God presents them live exciting lives for God.

I dislike being around negative people. In fact, if there is any way out of it, I will get away from negative people. If there's no way out of it, I'll find a way out. I like to think about the things that are true. We must examine every true reason why something will work out the way God intended for it to work out. I love spending time pondering upon the noble people and noble things that I'm associated with. I like to think about the things that are just and good. Pure hearted people are some of my favorite people in the world to be around because they have no hidden motives or agendas. You never have to figure out what they really mean or what they're thinking. They are pure hearted and honest. All of God's motives are pure and true. We must learn to meditate on lovely things. I mean, really it's a lot better than thinking about ugly things. I love a good report! Give me some good news. Tell me what's good in your life today. Tell me how that God-given destiny is working out for you. With God there are always good reports.

In every circumstance and situation of your life, you can talk about the good or you can talk about the bad. Every person that you meet, you can say good things about them or bad things about them. Today, choose to focus on the good report. If there is anything virtuous, think about those things. In every situation, talk about what is virtuous. Whenever you're around noble people who are praiseworthy, speak positively about them. Give out a compliment and speak life over people. I always want to be remembered as a person who changed the atmosphere whenever I walked in the room. I want to be someone who is true and noble. I want to be just, pure hearted, and talk about things that are of good report. If you always meditate and think upon the good things in life and don't focus on the bad, you will accomplish more. By meditating on good things, you will not be afraid to step out for God because something may not work. Focus on the good and allow God to get you a step closer to your God-given destiny.

WALKING IN KINGDOM POWER

Devotion 56

Jeremiah 29:12-13, "Then you will call upon Me and go and pray to Me, and I will listen to you. And you will seek Me and find Me, when you search for Me with all your heart." (NKJV)

Seekers of God will become children of destiny. Jeremiah 29:12-13 are scriptures that will drive you into your prayer room with great reverence, honor and expectancy with the guarantee that you will find the Lord. God promises that when you go to the place of prayer and lift up your voice that He will gladly answer you. He promises that every time we cry out, He hears our voice. God's heart is overjoyed when His children make the effort to go into that private place of prayer, shut out the world and call out to Him, their heavenly Father. God promises that He will be waiting eagerly to respond to your call. The Lord promises to always be found by us.

When you seek God with your entire heart, what you will find is exactly what you were seeking for. You will find the perfect plan and will that God has for your life. You will find the restoring power of God Almighty to put you back on your journey to your destiny. You will find encouragement from the Holy Spirit to try that God-given dream again. Finances will come in to help launch your business. When you seek, those people that you have been praying for to come back to the Lord will come running back to the Lord. When we pray and really believe that God is about to do everything that He said He would, our hearts and minds will be put at rest with Heaven's perspective.

We lift up our voices because we know that God is the only one that can change the circumstances and situations in our lives. Your Father takes great pleasure in moving all of Heaven and earth to show Himself strong on your behalf. God will remove things out of your way and place your necessities in your path. He will make a way where there seems to be no way and God will bring your breakthrough in just the right time. You are one call to the Lord away from having everything turn around for you. So cry out to the Lord and allow Him to set you back on the path to completing your God-given destiny.

WALKING IN KINGDOM POWER

Devotion 57

Proverbs 8:17, "I love those who love me, and those who seek me diligently will find me." (NKJV)

The love of God has no limit and no measure. The heights of God's love goes to the highest point and the depths of His love goes to the deepest points imaginable. His love is always willing and waiting for His children. God wants us to seek Him diligently with all of our heart because He has great promises of destiny for all of us. The key is that God must completely have our heart. Just like in Genesis 1:26-28, God gave man dominion over the earth because God wanted a day-to-day conversation with man to help guide and lead them. God would come down during the cool of the day to meet with Adam and Eve because He wanted to speak with them about their day-to-day life. God desires to be intricately involved in all of your lives. God cares about the details. The Scripture says that when we diligently seek God we will find Him. Many people are not walking in the fullness of their destiny because are trying to seek their own will not their Creator.

Deuteronomy 4:29 says, "But from there you will seek the Lord your God, and you will find Him if you seek Him with all your heart and with all your soul." Again, God is promising that when you daily seek after Him, He will reveal all the plans and purposes that He has before you. You will start to walk in your daily destiny and have a daily journey with God that you love and cherish. The Lord will speak dreams to you and make them come to pass. He will put a vision before you and you will watch it unravel day-by-day before your eyes. This will cause you to seek Him more each day, with all of your heart, mind and soul. The plan of God for His children is that they will walk daily with Him, through the good times and the bad and with God they will make it through anything. God has strategies and plans in Heaven that He is ready to release upon His children to carry them out. Let's be found seeking the Lord, and allow Him to give us daily steps towards the destiny that He has planned for us.

WALKING IN KINGDOM POWER

Devotion 58

James 1:6, "But let him ask in faith, with no doubting, for he who doubts is like a wave of the sea driven and tossed by the wind." (NKJV)

When God gives us the revelation of a new season in our life, a window into our destiny, or an adventure to take, we must never doubt Him. Our heavenly Father has never lied, nor will he, because His words are true. We must draw so close to God so we never mistake His voice for another. We will not have confusion when we know His voice. When we know God intimately, His voice is unmistakable. There is no voice like the voice of God. When the Lord reveals another step toward your destiny, never have fear or doubt because God has called and He will always provide for you.

God's timing is impeccable. Many times during our waiting, He will produce the fruit of patience within us. When we allow God to take us through the full process, we grow in wisdom, understanding and knowledge about where we are going. Whenever you launch out toward your destiny and attacks of the enemy, jealous friends, and critical peers come your way, if you are not grounded by the Spirit and the Word of God, you will be tossed around like a boat on a raging sea. When trials and test come your way, let them encourage you that you are on the right path. The devil never goes to war where there are no spoils.

James 1:2-3 says, "My brethren, count it all joy when you fall into various trials, knowing that the testing of your faith produces patience." (NKJV) Many times trials and test are like a mile marker on the road toward our destiny. Hard times can sometimes be signs that prove you are on your way toward your God-given destiny. Just like on a long journey, sometimes you stop refuel, stretch, take a small break and get right back on the road to your destination. The bigger the attack, the bigger your destiny is. When the enemy comes in and roars, remember our God is the lion of Judah. He has the loudest roar! Your daily encouragement is found in spending time with the Lord. He's like your daily dispatcher, lining you out for the journey ahead. Stay close to the voice of God and He will guide your steps to the destiny that He has for you.

WALKING IN KINGDOM POWER

Devotion 59

Proverbs 15:22, "Without counsel plans go astray, but in the multitude of counselors they are established." (NKJV)

God is faithful to always bring the right counsel alongside you to help steward the destiny that He has placed within you. There are many times in your life when you will have many mentors around you. Then there will be other times when it seems you have none. There can be times you have many peers that are running alongside you. There will be times you will feel you're running alone. But God always knows what you need in each season. Remember God puts certain people in your life for a reason, a season or lifetime. Many times you will have someone in your life for a reason. These people are there to teach you one specific thing to help you on the road to your destiny. There other times God brings people in your life for a season. Seasonal people are there for you to pick up certain traits or glean from their wisdom. Sometimes you learn what not to do by watching the seasonal people in your life. Then there will be very few people in your life who are with you for a lifetime. These are people who are always there whenever you need them. God will always provide the right wisdom and training you need to accomplish the destiny He has laid before you. It might not always look like you thought it would look but it will always be right.

Many times in the natural you will look around and say, "Lord, it seems I have no peers or mentors." This is a good sign because during these times you will learn to lean on the Holy Spirit for guidance and direction. Sometimes in life we will be in a wilderness or a cave season. These seasons are meant to take things out of our DNA that do not need to be there. Desert seasons will also draw us closer to the things of God. Many times we glean from mentors and friends so much that we neglect the power and presence of the Holy Spirit. Our God wants our time and attention and he will move people out of your life to make sure you stay close to Him. Holy Spirit's guidance and leading is crucial to our lives. We must seek daily counsel from the Holy Spirit and listen to the right counselors that God has placed in our paths. By using this wisdom, you will complete your God-given destiny.

WALKING IN KINGDOM POWER

Devotion 60

John 7:37-38, "Jesus said "If anyone thirsts, let him come to Me and drink. He who believes in Me, as the Scripture has said, out of his heart will flow rivers of living water."

What Jesus is offering in John 7:37-38 is the perfect picture of God providing life and destiny to every person who comes to Him. He starts off by asking if anyone is thirsty, then ends the Scripture with promising not only living water but that living water will flow from you. Jesus is offering people so much hope, salvation and destiny in just this one simple statement.

Today, many people are thirsty. There are countless lost people looking for what they cannot find. Jesus says, "When you believe in Me, you will find what you're looking for. Then you will have the ability to go show people and tell people about this living water you found." I love the fact that living water comes out of the heart because your heart is made up of both your soul and your spirit. I also love that Jesus promises not just one river but many rivers will flow from anyone who believes in Him. When you come to Jesus, you will find your purpose and you will be so filled with destiny that you will no longer be thirsty. Instead you will have rivers flowing out of your heart.

It does not take a river to quench thirst. Thirst could be satisfied with a simple glass of water. But this is the destiny that God has laid before us: so much more than we even ask for! Mere men want to be satisfied with something small and natural that will soon be gone in a day. After a glass of water, you will soon be thirsty again but God's desire is to sustain you! He doesn't want to just quench your thirst for one day, but He wants to bring forth rivers out of you that will satisfy you for a lifetime.

The size of rivers compared to one drink shows how much that God has stored up for those that are willing to lay down their lives for Him. When we get the visual picture that Jesus is offering so much more than salvation, we will begin to see our walk with God differently. Yes, salvation is enough but my God always gives more than enough! In these scriptures, Jesus states once you have a drink of His living water you will never thirst for anything else again. God wants you to go out with the power and authority that He gives you and take those rivers of living water everywhere you go on and to every person that you come in contact with.

Your region needs the rivers that are about to flow out of you. The rivers of God you release in your geographical location are vital. Your walk with God should be an overflowing river rushing into the city and region you are currently planted in. People will be drawn to you just to be able to drink from your river. Allow God to shape you and mold you daily so that you can release the river of God and fulfill your destiny!